1914

THE METHODIST

THE METHODIST

A Study in Discipleship

BY

HENRY CARTER

Author of
'THE CHURCH AND THE NEW AGE'

LONDON

CHARLES H. KELLY

25·35 City Road, and 26 Paternoster Row, E.C.

First Edition, 1914

THE 'FELLOWSHIP' LIBRARY

VOLUME I

This series of books is issued by a group of friends who meet at intervals for fellowship in thought and prayer. They are united by a common aim and by a common outlook upon life, but, as is natural, with respect to detailed application of principles the conclusions of each writer will not always represent those of the entire group.

The volumes may be few or many. Additions to the series will be furnished only as points of view are gained which, it is thought, may prove suggestive in the light of present-day difficulties and opportunities.

CONTENTS

CHAPTER I

TWO CENTURIES

Let us take a nearer view . . . of that great work of God among the children of men, which we are used to express by one word, 'Christianity'; not as it implies a set of opinions, a system of doctrines, but as it refers to men's hearts and lives.

JOHN WESLEY,
Sermon preached at St. Mary's, Oxford, before the University, August 24, 1744.

CHAPTER I

TWO CENTURIES

WHAT is the true Rule of Life for the modern disciple of Jesus?

A clear picture of Christian discipleship in the beginning is given in the New Testament writings, but the first Christian century and the twentieth are poles apart in their modes of living. Even the nineteenth and the twentieth are scarcely within speaking distance, so rapidly do we move from ways familiar to our fathers. In one generation the world has passed almost unawares into a new age, a new realm of thought and action.

Moral perplexities abound, personal, national, racial. The great root questions are laid bare again. What is the

meaning of human life? its purpose?
its destiny? Especially, what are the
authentic marks of a *Christian* life
to-day? Single out, for the sake of
definiteness, these three cases : a man's
customary use of time, his estimate of
money, his social responsibilities as
neighbour and citizen. What is the
present duty of the disciple of Jesus
in respect of each?

The question is as urgent as it is
difficult to answer. On the march
through new country, who can instruct
his comrade? We have not passed
this way heretofore. None the less
the men of to-day are not left without
witness of the will of Christ. He was
the Commander of the men of yesterday. There have been other eras than
this in which men lost sight of their
fathers' landmarks, and sought and
found a way through a land untrodden.
The conquering spirit of the past was
the Spirit of Jesus, deathless, unchang-
ing. Out of the annals of the past we
may learn the bidding of the one

Teacher and Guide for pilgrims of
to-day.

I

This is not the first generation called
to witness swift and decisive world-
wide change.   The Wesleys, and the
companies of the people called Methodists who gathered around them in the
eighteenth century, felt the pressure of
an age curiously parallel with our own.
They, like ourselves, saw the passing
of an old world-order ; like us, they
lived in the presence of the new and
the perplexing.

It is of more than historical interest,
it is of immediate importance, to note
the nearness of the parallel.

Consider three grave facts which
confront and challenge the Christian
thinker of the present day : the Social
Uprising at home and abroad ; the
shaking of the nations, with the re-
curring menace of war on a colossal
scale ; the renascence of Asia.   These

form the foreground of modern life.
In what varying degrees they affect
us none can say. Now the one, then
another, absorbs public interest. Together they represent the forces
changing the course of human history.
In the presence of them we are called
to develop a type of Christian discipleship which shall be God's living answer
to the needs of the new age.

Each of these three momentous
facts had its counterpart in Wesley's
century, and it was in face of them
that the first Methodists wrought out
a fresh interpretation of the Christian
' Way.'

The Social Uprising, the revolt
against underpay and overtoil, the
claim for a just share in the amenities
of life, is central and commanding for
us. We have seen in recent years, in
Britain, labour and capital at war,
and docks and railways and coalfields
—the muscles of a modern State—
paralysed ; in Ireland, the proud city
of Dublin laid waste by industrial

strife ; in South Africa, Government
and organized labour in fierce combat.
Wesley witnessed the writing of earlier
chapters of the story of social unrest.
The roots of our industrial troubles are
in his century. Between 1738 and
1791, the opening and closing years
of his evangelical ministry, are to be
placed the beginnings of the Industrial
Revolution. Invention called the
machine into industry, and hand labour
lost its value ; the factory system
began ; wage rates fell, and the
economic standard of life for manual
workers fell also. In rural areas en-
closures by the landed gentry were
depriving the labourer of his common
rights of tillage and pasturage. On the
other hand, large new populations
were settling on the coalfields of the
Midlands and the North. England
was in the full tide of change from
agricultural to manufacturing activities.
Moreover, 1789 was the memorable
year of the French Revolution. To a
watchful and eager student of life like

John Wesley, the stress and shock of social and political change were intensely vivid.

The parallel is even closer in international relations. The peril and shame of immense armaments, the periodic imminence of war, and the actual conflicts which have stained the soil of Europe, Asia, and Africa since the twentieth century opened, make up our skein of racial troubles ; yet these are more than equalled by the tangle of wars between England and France which fill the histories of the eighteenth century. Midway in Wesley's career came the Seven Years' War, reversing for all time the position of the two Empires in India and North America.

The renascence of Asia may well prove the most momentous of all changes. India, Japan, China—to name these is to state the problem in its vastest dimensions. One half of the human race, which till yesterday slumbrously faced the past, to-day

awakes race-conscious and insurgent.
What shall the future of Asia be?
Wesley's question differed only in one
word: What shall the future of
America be? The continent of Cabot
and Columbus filled his horizon. For
two years he toiled as missionary in
Georgia. He followed with close and
painful interest the events which led
to the Declaration of American Inde-
pendence in 1776. He sent Methodist
preachers to the American Colonies in
1769, and in 1784 ordained Coke a
Superintendent of the Methodist
Societies in the ' disentangled ' Repub-
lic. America to Wesley, Asia to us.
The problem is one. It is the problem
of the religious history of a continent.

II

Striking and suggestive is the likeness between the world-drama of our
age and that in the presence of which
the leaders of the early Methodists
achieved their victory for Christ and

B

His Kingdom; for they won, and the righteousness which exalteth a nation won through them.

Not less significant is the likeness between our problem of personal discipleship and theirs. It is easy to see how notable changes in the outward characteristics of life may mould the actual character of life, where life is impressionable. All that has yet been said can be summed up in a sentence: we are wrestling for wealth, class against class, while the whole world is opening its treasures at our feet. That is the meaning of the Social Uprising; it is a struggle for a juster division of the means to live and to enjoy. That is the result of the impact of nation on nation, race on race; the resources of every land are revealed to each.

Two types of life are distinguishable already amidst the confusions of the age.

There is a new pagan amongst us who lives to get, to spend, to satisfy his fleshly longings. Whether he works to earn, or wastes what others earn, he lives frankly and unashamedly for himself. The fresh gifts of the universe minister to his self-indulging appetites. To eat and drink and flaunt gay clothes; to please the eye and ear with new sensation; to make of bodily desires a god, and pay homage at that shrine— such is his scheme of life; such are the streets, such is the temple, where the new pagan wanders and worships. The narrow streets of his desire shut him in; he sees no vision.

The second type is known by varying names: a good citizen, a kindly neighbour, an earnest churchman. Whatever his name or creed or station, this is the mark of the man—he serves his fellows. His touch with the Church may be intimate as a confessed follower of Jesus; or the Christian element in him, the will to serve, may be his share of our heritage from the Christian centuries. As the new pagan is the chief peril of modern society, so this man at his best is society's main

hope. His social worth is Christian
in its source ; in him, therefore, the
Church can touch the age redemptively. Viewed in its human aspect,
the vital work of the Church and the
vital worth of her work is represented
in this man. The Church is to save
the race by gifts of living goodness,
men and women unselfish, sacrificial,
spiritual. And the problem of men and
women thus minded is to make real in
common life the thoughts and teachings
of Jesus. They are to obey Him in
commerce and home, in politics, and
in the Christian company. They are
to obey Him without quibble and
without limit. They are to attempt
this in a world where old things are in
decay, whose atmosphere is change.
Amidst the unfamiliar they are to prepare the way of the Lord. In the face
of a new paganism they are to witness
to a new interpretation of Christian
discipleship ; broad enough to over-
spread life public and personal, racial
and national ; deep enough to cut its

own channel through the hard soils of indifference and greed.

What has been said of England of the eighteenth century shows how closely parallel was the task of the Wesleys. There is a passage in John Wesley's *Farther Appeal to Men of Reason and Religion* which states in retrospect his view of the power of the Methodist preaching and practice when it broke on England at the first. The Puritan revival of the seventeenth century had spent its force. The nation, morally and spiritually, was in a Slough of Despond.

Wesley recounts the gross sins of that generation, intemperance, lewdness, violence, and so forth, and continues : ' Just at this time, when we wanted little of filling up the measure of our iniquities, two or three clergymen of the Church of England[1] began vehemently to call sinners to repentance. In two or three years they had sounded

[1] The reference is, of course, to George Whitefield and to John and Charles Wesley.

the alarm to the utmost borders of the
land.   Many thousands gathered together to hear them ; and in every
place where they came many began to
show such a concern for religion as they
never had done before. A stronger
impression was made on their minds
of the importance of things eternal, and
they had more earnest desires of serving
God than they had ever had from their
earliest childhood.   Thus did God begin
to draw them toward Himself. . . .

‘ And from hence sprung fruits meet
for repentance. The drunkard com-
menced sober and temperate ; the
whoremonger abstained from adultery
and fornication ; the unjust from
oppression and wrong. He that had
been accustomed to curse and swear
for many years now swore no more.
The sluggard began to work with his
hands, that he might earn his own
bread. The miser learned to deal his
bread to the hungry, and to cover the
naked with a garment. Indeed, the
whole form of their life was changed.

They had " left off doing evil, and learned to do well." '

The new discipleship overcame the new paganism. It is of immediate import to us, whose task is as urgent and so strangely similar, to study the fashion of the discipleship that triumphed thus.

CHAPTER II

THE GREAT TRADITION

We see, on every side, either men of no religion at all, or men of a lifeless, formal religion. We are grieved at the sight; and should greatly rejoice, if by any means we might convince some that there is a better religion to be attained—a religion worthy of God that gave it. And this we conceive to be no other than love; the love of God and of all mankind; the loving God with all our heart, and soul, and strength, as having first loved us, as the fountain of all the good we have received, and of all we ever hope to enjoy; and the loving every soul which God hath made, every man on earth, as our own soul.

JOHN WESLEY,
An Earnest Appeal to Men of Reason and Religion, 1743.

CHAPTER II

THE GREAT TRADITION

THEY were a little company of men and women, gathered chiefly from the poor and unlearned. Their bond of union was religious. The people called Methodists united ' in order to pray together, to receive the word of exhortation, and to watch over one another in love, that they might help each other to work out their salvation.' They had a charge to keep. They sang :

> To serve the present age,
>   My calling to fulfil :
> Oh, may it all my powers engage
>   To do my Master's will !

But *to serve the present age* ! How could they ? The framework of democratic government—Parish and Town and County Councils, and a Parliament open to the labouring man—was undreamt of in their day. Telegraph and telephone, railway and steamship, a daily Press, and a cheap literature of economics, all belonged to the future. The world-drama, as their leaders saw it, a drama of social change and conflict, of French wars in Canada and India, of the new nation arising in America, was, we might almost say, hidden from their eyes. And yet they served their age, richly and redemptively—saved their age it may be. How ?

I

Their service grew out of their experience, out of their knowledge of God and of the needs of men.

They had rediscovered God. Longing to flee from the wrath to come, to be saved from their sins, they found Him in Christ as Saviour. Conscious of a present salvation, they strove to live as men freed from the guilt and power of sin. Inevitably their life conformed to a certain type. Wesley said of the use of money that the Christian ought calmly and seriously to inquire, ' In expending this, am I acting according to my character ? ' The early Methodists were called to act according to their character in all things, in keeping with their distinctive quality as Christians. They developed an uncommon way of living. They observed a rule of life. The sneer was a fact : they were ' methodists.'

English life of the eighteenth century was, broadly speaking, rough, hearty, garish, self-pleasing. The authentic Methodist way of living was disciplined, tenderly affectioned, modest in self-gratification, unsparing in duty to God and neighbour. The primitive Methodist lived for the joy and adventure of the Kingdom. He served his generation and its Master with a glad heart and free.

The Wesleys, John and Charles, were
the pathfinders. We can trace their
trail even in Georgia as pioneers of a
new discipline of the devout life. But
it was on a later night in London that
John lighted on the new way into
which for fifty years and more he was
to guide thousands.

He had gone to a religious society in
Aldersgate Street, ' where one was
reading Luther's preface to the Epistle
to the Romans.' While the reader
was ' describing the change which God
works in the heart through faith in
Christ,' runs John Wesley's record of
the memorable hour, ' I felt my heart
strangely warmed. I felt I did trust
in Christ, Christ alone for salvation ;
and an assurance was given me that He
had taken away *my* sins, even *mine*,
and saved *me* from the law of sin and
death.'

Then he goes on to add significant
words : ' I began to pray with all my
might for those who had in a more
especial manner despitefully used me

and persecuted me.' The great assurance and the great affection kindled in the same hour ; for to discover God as Saviour was to discern man as neighbour. So, concludes Wesley, ' I then testified openly to all there what I now first felt in my heart.'

That was on May 24, 1738.

II

In 1743 the *Rules* to govern the Societies of the people called Methodists were issued.[1] Assurance and affection, sureness of God and service of man, are the notes of this charter of the original Methodist experience.

The little document shows a new conviction cleaving a new way through life. In contact with eighteenth-century England, the Methodist was to do no harm, to avoid evil in every kind ;

[1] A few changes were made by Wesley in the numerous later editions of the *Rules*. These are specified in Tyerman, *Life and Times of Wesley*, vol. i. pp. 430–1. The *Rules* are quoted in their final form in the succeeding chapters.

and the evils most generally practised were set out in plain speech. He was to do good, of every possible sort and as far as possible to all men; and ministries to men's bodies and souls and temporal circumstances were specified. He was to attend upon all the ordinances of God.

This code of duty, not for duty's sake but at love's behest, became the standard by which the true Methodist was distinguished from the false. The *Rules* were given to a member as he joined the Methodist Society. Habitually to break any of them was a sufficient ground for the expulsion of the offender. ' We will admonish him of the error of his ways; we will bear with him for a season. But then if he repent not, he hath no more place among us.' The type of life was recognizable. To depart from it, wilfully and constantly, was to cease to be a Methodist. The Society that had strength to exclude the evildoer had strength to overcome the evil.

The way of life of the first Methodists is recorded in the *Rules*. It will be well worth while to state in terms of to-day the spiritual and social significance of the document. Its value is not alone that the *Rules* still stand as the authoritative test of Methodist experience and practice, though that is true. The real value of the document to us is this. It is the record of a recovery of the true witness of Christian discipleship in one of the world's decisive eras. A new age sprang its challenge on Christ's Church. For answer, a company of spiritual adventurers arose who through faith subdued kingdoms and wrought righteousness. Here is written the manner of their living. Incompetent and ignorant as the learned judged them, they won the day for God. Britain, passing through the earlier stages of the Industrial Revolution, found its horrors mitigated by multitudes of loving hearts whose days were spent in doing good. The verdict of

C

history credits the Methodist Revival with England's immunity from terrors akin to those of the French Revolution. The continent of North America became not pagan, but the home of a mighty Christianity of which Methodism was the fiery herald.

This is the great tradition handed down from our fathers, a tradition of triumph. The Wesleys and their fellow Methodists accepted the challenge of their age. They developed a new way of life to meet its claims. They arraigned evil baldly and boldly. They wrought good without ceasing. They adhered to the ordinances of God. They trusted in Him and were not confounded.

CHAPTER III

A MODERN STUDY OF THE 'RULES'

1. THE CHRISTIAN NEGATIVE

*This book, it chalketh out before thine eyes
The man that seeks the everlasting prize.*

*This book will make a traveller of thee,
If by its counsel thou wilt rulèd be.*

JOHN BUNYAN,
' The Author's Apology,' *The Pilgrim's
Progress.*

CHAPTER III

A MODERN STUDY OF THE ' RULES '

I. THE CHRISTIAN NEGATIVE

EACH Methodist Society was ' a company of men having the form, and seeking the power, of godliness.' They were united to ' help each other to *work out* their salvation.' That was their aim, precise and definite. Salvation was not a theological label, but a way of living. That it might be the more easily discerned whether its members were working out in practice the principles of their new life, a Society was divided into smaller companies, or Classes, each under the guidance of a Leader.

Only one condition was required in those who sought admission to the Society : ' A desire to flee from the wrath to come, to be saved from their sins.' ' But,' the *Rules* continue, with fine insistence on the essential union of Christianity with character, ' where-ever this '—the desire to be saved from sins—' is really fixed in the soul, it will be shown by its fruits. It is therefore expected of all who continue therein ' —that is, in the Methodist Society— ' that they should continue to evidence their desire of salvation,

> *FIRST*, By doing no harm.
> *SECONDLY*, By doing good.
> *THIRDLY*, By attending upon all the ordinances of God.'

Here are, in truth, the Christian Negative, the Christian Positive, and the secret of the Christian Dynamic, set out with certain of their spiritual and social implications. We turn to these to feel their force afresh.

I

The Christian Negative—'Doing No Harm'

The full statement of abstinences from evil is arresting. Under the general negative, 'doing no harm,' Wesley places, after his practical fashion, specific instances. The Methodist was to continue to evidence his desire of salvation,

FIRST, By doing no harm, by avoiding evil in every kind ; especially that which is most generally practised.   Such is

The taking the name of God in vain ;

The profaning the day of the Lord, either by doing ordinary work thereon, or by buying or selling ;

Drunkenness ; buying or selling spirituous liquors, or drinking them, unless in cases of extreme necessity ;

Fighting, quarrelling, brawling ; brother going to law with brother ; returning evil for evil, or railing for railing ; the using many words in buying or selling ;

The buying or selling uncustomed goods ;

The giving or taking things on usury; i.e. unlawful interest;

Uncharitable or unprofitable conversation; particularly speaking evil of magistrates or of ministers;

Doing to others as we would not they should do unto us;

Doing what we know is not for the glory of God; as—

    The putting on of gold or costly apparel;

    The taking such diversions as cannot be used in the name of the LORD JESUS;

    The singing those songs, or reading those books which do not tend to the knowledge or love of God;

Softness, and needless self-indulgence;

Laying up treasures upon earth;

Borrowing without a probability of paying; or taking up goods without a probability of paying for them.

The immediate impression as one reads this eighteenth-century Rule of Life in the light of its century is that of challenge and combat. The evil *most generally practised* was that from which the Methodist was to abstain. ' The way to heaven is singularity all over,' wrote Wesley; ' if you move but one step towards God, you are not as other men are.'[1]

It was an age intolerant of moral restraint. The common contemporary way of life in England was to do what was right in one's own eyes, to gratify one's own desires at whatever cost. The Christian name was far from being an index to a Christian character. The list of evils 'most generally practised' is witness to that. In face of a common disregard of moral sanctions, the Wesleys enjoined upon the Methodist Societies self-discipline, in the fear and for the love of God. At the least the life of the Methodist should run full tilt against conventional, everyday wrong-doing. At its highest it should represent a constant, intelligent self-restraint in face of the Kingdom's multiplying claims.

To say this is not to idealize these our fathers in the Faith. It is because they were men of like passions with us,

[1] Eleventh Discourse *Upon our Lord's Sermon on the Mount.*

wrestling against the love of ease, of
money, and of the praise of men, as we
needs must wrestle ; warring against
coarse lusts and common hates, as is
our bounden duty ; winning here and
baffled there, yet baffled to fight better ;
of our clay, though shaped of God—it
is because they were as we are, and the
victors among them came to be what
we ought to be, that this record of their
way of life concerns us vitally.

A fourfold grouping of the abstinences from evil will bring us nearest
to the mind of Wesley, and show the
development of his thought in this
statement of the Christian Negative.
Necessarily he wrote for his own
generation. The evils most generally
practised in the England of the
eighteenth century figure here. Nevertheless, to bring them into relation
to the life of our century requires
change in phrase rather than in fact.
The ancient entail of evil is still
unbroken.

II

First, then, come sins which were, we may say, already on the ' black list ' of his day.

These were acts generally condemned by professors of religion, and recognized as evil if not repudiated as evil. Such were :

> *Taking the name of God in vain ;*
> *Profaning the day of the Lord, either*
>   *by doing ordinary work thereon,*
>   *or by buying and selling ;*
> *Drunkenness ;*
> *Fighting, quarrelling, brawling.*

Three trenchant Tracts from Wesley's pen, *A Word to a Swearer, A Word to a Sabbath-Breaker*, and *A Word to a Drunkard*, indict, reason, and plead with those who thus affront the sanctities of life, human and divine.

Of the rightful use of the day of the Lord there will be much to say later when we explore the secret of the Christian Dynamic, 'attending upon all the ordinances of God.'

III

Next are named practices that were not on the 'black list' of eighteenth-century Christianity, but which Wesley instinctively knew to be breaches of the Golden Rule of Christian love.

Two of these he exposed by laying bare the roots of evils commonly recognized as such, drunkenness and brawling.

Drunkenness, as the prolific parent of misery and crime, was discreditable. That was agreed. What, then, of the traffic in spirituous liquors, and the habit of liquor drinking? These too should be discredited, for cause and effect are morally inseparable. So Wesley set under the Christian Negative not drunkenness alone, but also

Buying and selling spirituous liquors,

> *or drinking them, unless in cases
> of extreme necessity.*

The words call for emphasis rather than
exposition. The famous paragraph in
his sermon on *The Use of Money* is
the best comment :

' Neither may we gain by hurting our
neighbour in his body. Therefore we
may not sell anything which tends to
impair health. Such is, eminently, all
that liquid fire, commonly called drams,
or spirituous liquors. It is true, these
may have a place in medicine ; they
may be of use in some bodily disorders ;
although there would rarely be occasion for them, were it not for the unskil-
fulness of the practitioner. Therefore,
such as prepare and sell them only for
this end may keep their conscience
clear. But who are they ? Who prepare them only for this end ? Do you
know ten such distillers in England ?
Then excuse these. But all who sell
them in the common way, to any that
will buy, are poisoners general. They

murder His Majesty's subjects by wholesale, neither does their eye pity or spare. They drive them to hell, like sheep.

' And what is their gain? Is it not the blood of these men? Who, then, would envy their large estates and sumptuous palaces? A curse of God is in their gardens, their walks, their groves ; a fire that burns to the nethermost hell! Blood, blood is there : the foundation, the floor, the walls, the roof, are stained with blood ! '

Strong drink desecrates body, mind, and soul ; therefore the disciple of Jesus ought neither to touch nor traffic in it.[1]

After the manner of the Sermon on the Mount, which he delighted to

[1] The *Rules*, drafted in 1743, date nearly a century before the Total Abstinence Movement began in England. The ' Seven Men of Preston ' signed their famous pledge in 1832 ' to abstain from all liquors of an intoxicating quality, whether ale, porter, wines, or ardent spirits, except as medicines.' It scarcely needs to be pointed out that the moral ground for Wesley's repudiation of ' spirituous,' i.e. distilled liquors, is, as we have taken it to be, a sure footing

expound, Wesley also opened out the meaning of acts of 'fighting, quarrelling, brawling.' Openly to brawl was unchristian. Then what of the contentious spirit? Were not root and fruit of the same tree? Ought Christian men to prosecute one another, to retaliate in deed or word, to give occasion for anger by misrepresentation in business, by tricks of trade? Assuredly not. Hence the Christian Negative must include,

> *Brother going to law with brother :*
> *Returning evil for evil, or railing*
> * for railing :*
> *The using many words in buying*
> * or selling.*

The last phrase covers a multitude of sins in business life to-day.

for the later reformers who also repudiated brewed liquors. Modern science declares alcohol to be a poison, and modern social research establishes by manifold proofs the fact that alcoholic liquors— whether brewed or distilled—grievously impair the powers of brain and body, and are a fruitful cause of crime, destitution, and disease.

Two other breaches of the Golden
Rule also relate to commerce :

*The buying or selling uncustomed
   goods ;*
*The giving or taking things on usury ;
   i.e. unlawful interest.*

If the average Christian conscience of
his day would not call these evils evil,
Wesley would and did.

His attitude to the traffic in uncustomed goods was characteristic.
Smuggling was so general as to have
become ' a kind of national failing.'
Even Adam Smith was an apologist for
the smuggler. Not so Wesley. No
fine language would make wrong right
for him. Smuggling, he says, ' is a
general robbery. It is, in effect, not
only robbing the King, but robbing
every honest man in the nation. For
the more the King's duties are dimin-
ished, the more the taxes must be
increased. And these lie upon us all.
. . . Therefore every smuggler is a

thief-general, who picks the pockets both of the King and all his fellow subjects. He wrongs them all.' So Wesley bade his Preachers ' speak tenderly, but earnestly and frequently of it, in every Society near the coasts ; and read to them, and diligently disperse among them, the *Word to a Smuggler*, the forceful tract just quoted, written by himself. ' Fear nothing,' he wrote Joseph Benson, in 1776, after Benson had put a smuggler out of the Methodist Society. ' Begin in the name of God and go through with the work. If only six will promise you to sin no more, leave only six in the Society.' It was drastic dealing. It meant that the Methodist way of life was a way of No-Compromise with evil, personal or public.

As with smuggling so with usury. The early Methodist teaching had no uncertain sound respecting any social duty. The sermon on *The Use of Money* should be read here also :

' We cannot, if we love every one as

D

ourselves, hurt any one in his substance. We cannot devour the increase
of his lands, and perhaps the lands and
houses themselves, by gaming, by
overgrown bills . . . or by requiring
or taking such interest as even the laws
of our country forbid.'

Modern applications of this teaching
lie right at hand. Clearly a doctrine
which bids men refrain from aught
that would 'hurt any one in his substance' forbids all forms of betting
and gambling. Just as clearly it
challenges the right to high dividends
won by the sweating or spoiling of
others.

IV

The Christian ethic in Wesley's hand
cut yet deeper. What made these
external acts heinous was that they
sprang from a self-centred, self-indulging habit of life.

An objector might say, ' But if you
forbid me to trade in liquors or

uncustomed goods, to take these short ways to wealth, I cannot become rich.' Wesley would answer, ' Why should you ? The word of Jesus was, " Lay not up for yourselves treasures upon earth." ' If the objector persisted, ' But in that case I cannot enjoy the ease and pleasures of the rich,' Wesley's reply would be, ' Neither is that your business if you are a Christian. A Christian's business is to seek first the Kingdom of God and His righteousness.'

That is to say, life to the understanding Methodist was a vocation. God was calling for immense exacting services. The stirring events of the century—rapid industrial change at home and the clash of empires abroad, insurgent America, and the new campaign of Christ in Britain—were voices of God to him. Storm voices, yet voices of command. A new England, a new nation across the Atlantic, the fabric of a new world, were rising in his generation. He must claim all for

God, win all for the obedience of the
Kingdom. ' Soldiers of Christ, arise ! '

The King's business required haste.
The new urgency drove Wesley back on
the simplicity of life as Jesus had conceived it. With a sufficiency of food,
clothing, and life's necessaries, the
Christian should be content ; his
strength should go into the primal
quest for righteousness. Envy, display,
and tender self-considerations meant
that life was moving from its true
centre. They were a waste of resources needed for purposes of the
Kingdom, and therefore were not for
the glory of God.

This is the origin and interpretation
of restrictive phrases in the *Rules*,
some of which to modern ears may
otherwise sound repellent. Rightly
understood, they are a part of the
discipline of Christ's soldiers on service.

Uncharitable or unprofitable con-
versation ; particularly speaking
evil of magistrates and ministers,

is a breach of the law of love stated in the succeeding sentence which forbids the ' Doing to others as we would not they should do unto us.' Wesley, fearlessly revolutionary in teaching, flung his shield over ' magistrates and ministers '—a noble revenge, for he suffered much at the hands of Justices and clergy.

Under the comprehensive phrase, ' Doing what we know is not for the glory of God,' is placed a group of habits which should be alien to Christ's campaigners :

> *The putting on of gold or costly apparel ;*
> *The taking such diversions as cannot be used in the name of the Lord Jesus ;*
> *The singing those songs or reading those books which do not tend to the knowledge or love of God.*

Vanity in ornament or dress, recreations which compromise the Christian character, and futile and fruitless reading mean money, time, and working-power lost to the Kingdom. ' All unnecessary expenses of this kind, whether small or great, are senseless and foolish. . . . Consider this more closely : Here are two ways proposed of laying out such a sum of money. I may lay it out in expensive apparel for myself, or in necessary clothing for my neighbour. The former will please my own eye, or that of others ; the latter will please God. Now suppose there were no more harm in one than in the other, in that which pleases man than in that which pleases God, is there as much good in it ? If they were equally innocent, are they equally wise ? . . . Let no needless expense hinder your being, *in the highest degree you possibly can*, " rich in good works, ready to distribute, willing to communicate." '[1]

From this point of view the next requirement is readily understood, the avoidance of

[1] John Wesley : *Advice to the People called Methodists with regard to Dress.*

Softness and needless self-indulgence.

'Softness' is a caustic word which 'needless self-indulgence' explains.

> *Borrowing without a probability of paying; or taking up goods without a probability of paying for them,*

is a practical ethical climax to the Methodist exposition of the Christian Negative, 'doing no harm.' 'Never think of being religious unless you are honest,' wrote Wesley in an 'Address to the Societies at Bristol.'

V

One phrase has been reserved for close and careful examination. It is fundamental to much that has preceded, and raises a problem central and crucial to-day :

Laying up treasures upon earth.

This was forbidden in the *Rules* to

the primitive Methodist, as it is forbidden in the New Testament to all Christians.

To settle one's attitude to money is to settle much beside. The rightful uses of time, and the right discharge of social responsibilities as neighbour and citizen, are bound up with the question of earning and spending. Examination at this point must therefore be thorough.

We encounter here a radical difference between the teaching and practice of Jesus and the everyday habit of most of His disciples. It is taken for granted now that industry and integrity have a right to hold the wealth they win, and that it is honourable to grow rich. Jesus said with emphasis, ' Lay not up for yourselves treasures upon the earth,' and, ' How hardly shall they that have riches enter into the Kingdom of God.' The common practice of modern Christianity, and the plainest meaning of the sayings of Jesus, are irreconcilable.

Wesley held tenaciously to the belief that Jesus meant exactly what He said, that it was the business of His disciple to shun riches, and that in doing so he would go far to make possible ' this strange sight, a Christian world.' Here, also, his life was of equal force with his word. As author and publisher he earned in later years an income which even now would rank him with the well-to-do ; yet he gave as he gained, and died a poor man.[1] If Wesley understood Jesus aright, do not we misunderstand Him ? In a serious attempt to restate the

[1] In a sermon on *The Danger of Riches* written in 1780 he says, ' Two-and-forty years ago. having a desire to furnish poor people with cheaper, shorter, and plainer books than any I had seen, I wrote many small tracts, generally a penny a-piece ; and afterwards several larger. Some of these had such a sale as I never thought of ; and, by this means, I unawares became rich. But I never desired or endeavoured after it. And now that it is come upon me unawares, I lay up no treasures upon earth ; I lay up nothing at all. . . . I cannot help leaving my books behind me whenever God calls me hence ; but, in every other respect, my own hands will be my executors.'

meaning of Christian discipleship this
perplexity may not be evaded. We
cannot but handle money, whether
earned, inherited, or given. The get-
ting and spending of money is a concern of every man. What is the
authentic Christian doctrine, the true
Christian practice, in this respect?

A preliminary and important objection to this inquiry is that it should be
social rather than personal, since the
methods which enable some to accumu-
late great riches are rooted in the
economic system of to-day. ' Change
the system if it is bad,' some say, ' but
do not blame individuals who have
no choice but to work under it.'

Few will question that notable economic changes in the distribution of
wealth lie ahead, and probably are not
far distant. The gulf between the
immense fortunes of the few and the
half-starved lot of the many is too
wide and too cruel to endure. The
tendency of legislation is one evidence
of that. Yet two considerations show

that the use of money is a personal as well as a public responsibility.

First, the fact that a few are fabulously rich, while the toil of multitudes wins them only the scantiest livelihood, means that self-interest has dictated and shaped the framework of commerce: but self-interest was not impersonal, it was personal ; anti-social relationships have grown up because anti-social men have shaped them. If a new economic order is to arise, social and just to all, a new type of man is needed, a citizen with widely differing ideas concerning money-getting and money-spending than prevail to-day.

In the second place, the beginnings of economic change are already visible. With no clear conception of an ideal social order, a transition from the unideal to the ideal has actually begun. The sheer misery of things as they are is forcing the State to ask how things ought to be, and to find or make a way thither. We live in the era of change. But we cannot wait until change is complete before our habits are moralized. We ought to be moral now. It is true that commerce and politics are very imperfect morally, and that the imperfections of the present economic system limit the freedom of the individual. Still, to the extent that we are free—and that is greater than self-interest usually admits—as disciples of Jesus we are under immediate obligation to earn and use money after a Christian fashion. One may go farther and say that in so far as we fail to do this we hold back the dawn. The perfect day will never come merely because men talk of it. It may if men live for it.

Directly the question of one's present attitude to money and the use of it is seriously faced, it will be seen that Wesley, in practice and preaching, took a simple, straight line through the jungle of difficulties. His doctrine of *Gain—Save—Give*, understood as he stated it, is concise, convincing, Christian.

Wesley began where we must begin, with the attitude of Jesus, and His earliest followers, to riches. Their teaching is neither scanty nor dubious, however little it has been taken into the world's working account.

'There is a new creation whenever a man comes to be in Christ; what is old is gone, the new has come.'[1] In respect of wealth, and what it can buy, the 'old' that Christ bids go is the belief that a man *owns* what he holds, and that life's main aim is to increase one's holding; the 'new' which Christ brings is a new standard of values, and a new practice in money matters.

The 'old' is repudiated by Jesus in His story of the Rich Landholder,[2] for instance. He ranked in popular estimation as a great owner. Jesus depicts him surveying proudly '*my* fruits,' '*my* barns,' '*my* corn,' '*my* goods,' and planning years of ease. Even so, nature itself denied his

[1] 2 Cor. v. 17 (Moffatt's translation).
[2] Luke xii. 16-21.

title to own ; it was ' the ground ' that
brought forth plentifully. He was not
creator, only cultivator ; nor sole
cultivator, for others had dug, and
planted, and reaped what he purposed
to enjoy. Paul would have challenged
him, as he challenged certain men of
Corinth, ' What hast thou that thou
didst not receive ? ' Whether from
nature, from the toil of others, or
through personal wit or strength, all
came originally from God. Paul's
Master gave the truth dramatic force :
while the rich man planned ease, out
of the silence came a Voice speaking
naked truth, ' Fool, this night is thy
soul required of thee ; and the things
which thou hast prepared, whose shall
they be ? ' There can be no appeal
for any of us from that sentence. It
lays bare reality. No man owns. ' The
earth is the Lord's, and the fullness
thereof.' There is a place for each in
His scheme ; when we drop the folly
of posing as owners, and the madness
of counting silver and gold, houses or

fields, the prizes of life, then the Sovereign and Owner of all can enrol and employ us as stewards, men and women in trust of what is His, for use at His direction.

This brings us to the ' new ' which Jesus proclaimed.

Luke's method of writing sets immediately after the story of the Rich Landholder Jesus' comments.

His disciples were, first, to accept a new standard of values. ' The life—the soul—is more than the food.' Better die than deny goodness. Righteousness is to be the supreme concern. Righteousness, to the mind of Jesus, was an immense affair ; it was racial, for it aimed to establish God's supremacy everywhere ; ' seek ye His Kingdom,' Jesus went on to say. The new standard is therefore plain ; it does not ask, Will this pay ? but, Is this right ? It establishes a new range of values : it does not sanction respect of men because they are rich, but only as they are good ; it does not lead to coveting, but to sacrifice for the Kingdom's sake; it does not highly estimate subtle schemes for gaining riches, but would have men 'experts in good, innocents in evil.' 'Let your turn of mind be free from the love of money,'[1] is a fair rendering of the new standard of values as applied to finance.

Acceptance of the new standard leads to a new practice in money matters. As was the rich landholder, summed up by God at the last as a fool, 'so,' said Jesus, 'is he that layeth up treasure for himself, and is not rich toward God.' The comment presupposes His actual precept, recorded by Matthew, and cited by Wesley, 'Lay not up for yourselves treasures upon the earth.'

It is here that Wesley made contribution to Christian ethics. He showed how this hard saying of Jesus could be applied in a commercial age. It is altogether noteworthy that Wesley

[1] Heb. xiii. 5 (R.V. margin).

proclaimed his teaching, far and wide, at a time when new mechanical agencies were vastly increasing the national wealth. In his youth the Darbys, father and son, discovered how to use pit-coal in smelting metals ; the casual reader of Wesley's *Journals* cannot fail to see how conspicuously the new populations on the coalfields at Kingswood, in the Midlands, and around Newcastle figure in Wesley's England. In 1769 James Watt patented his condensing steam-engine, and steam entered the service of man. In the next two decades a group of brilliant inventions by Hargreaves, Arkwright, Crompton, and Cartwright turned the spinning and weaving of cotton from handicrafts into machine industries, and dotted the northern valleys with cotton-mills. In that age of swift change, when the command of capital meant power to increase wealth on a scale unprecedented in home industry, Wesley raised again the cry of Jesus against the amassing of personal fortunes. Had

E

his message been heeded, the tyrannies and horrors which accompanied the Industrial Revolution in Britain would have been averted.[1] We are paying the price to-day for economic sins of yesterday.

What, precisely, was Wesley's way of turning into everyday practice this precept of Jesus, ' Lay not up for yourselves treasures upon the earth ' ?

Not idleness. Charles Wesley set the Methodists singing,

> Their earthly task who fail to do
> Neglect their heavenly business too.

Not a refusal to use the new powers with which invention arms man. Wesley would have joined heartily in John Ellerton's ascription :

> Thine is the loom, the forge, the mart,
>   The wealth of land and sea,
> The worlds of science and of art
>   Revealed and ruled by Thee.

[1] See, e.g., the author's *The Church and the New Age*, pp. 3–6 and 59–76.

Not a decrying of money as unclean.
' Let the world be as corrupt as it will,
is gold or silver to blame ? ' he asks.
' The fault does not lie in the money,
but in them that use it. It may be used
ill : and what may not ? But it may
likewise be used well : it is full as
applicable to the best as to the worst
uses.'

Wesley gave his answer in three
simple directions :

> Gain all you can ;
> Save all you can ;
> Give all you can.

The three are one, and lose moral
significance unless so regarded. Woven
together, and used as Wesley used them
and urged their use, they are counsels
adequate to any situation. Their
meaning is worked out most fully in
the sermon on *The Use of Money*,
from which we must freely quote ;
though, as already stated, the daily
habit of Wesley is a continual
exposition of them. He needed a
working principle for his own guidance,

and fashioned these three counsels out of material quarried from the New Testament.

Gain all you can. ' We ought to gain all we can, without buying gold too dear, without paying for it more than it is worth.' Hence the frontiers of the right to gain are drawn decisively for the Christian.

(*a*) He ought not to gain at the expense of his own body. ' Whatever it is which reason or experience shows to be destructive of health or strength, that we may not submit to.' Wesley's illustrations sound curiously modern : he banned, as typical instances, gain at the cost of ' dealing much with arsenic,' or ' breathing an air tainted with streams of melting lead,' for these ' must at length destroy the finest constitution.'

(*b*) He ought not to gain at the expense of his own soul. This bans all businesses which ' will not afford a competent maintenance without cheating or lying ; or conformity to

some custom which is not consistent
with a good conscience . . . for, to
gain money, we must not lose our souls.'

(*c*) He ought not to gain at the
expense of his neighbour's substance.
His care for his own welfare is to be
matched by care for his neighbour,
whom he is to love as himself. ' We
cannot study to ruin our neighbour's
trade in order to advance our own.'
' None can gain by swallowing up his
neighbour's substance without gaining
the damnation of hell.'

(*d*) He ought not to gain at the
expense of his neighbour's body or soul.
' We may not sell anything which tends
to impair health.' We may not minister, ' either directly or indirectly, to
the unchastity or intemperance ' of our
neighbour. We may not ' play with
the lives or health of men.' On this
principle the *Rules* expressly forbade
the Methodist to sell spirituous liquors.
To sweat the poor by underpayment is
as plainly forbidden by it ; wage rates
must be just.

Within these limits—and what they
exclude is socially unrighteous—the
disciple of Jesus is free to gain all he
can. We may expand Wesley's First
Counsel, so as to mark its frontiers
as he drew them, thus :

> Gain all you can without hurt
> to body or soul, your own or
> your neighbour's.

Short cuts to wealth which are
vicious or unjust are barred to the
Christian ; none the less the more he
is a Christian the more surely will
he possess two credentials of success
in business, industry and integrity.
Wesley's call to ' honest industry ' is
too good not to quote : ' Lose no time.
If you understand yourself, and your
relation to God and man, you know you
have none to spare. . . . Never leave
anything till to-morrow which you
can do to-day. And do it as well as
possible. Do not sleep or yawn over
it ; put your whole strength to the
work. Spare no pains.'

While opportunities, educational and economic, are still very unequal, the will to work and the conscience to work honourably often lead to prosperity. Hence arises the question, How ought a Christian to handle his money? Whether wage-earner, trader, investor, or inheritor, whether rich or poor, what principle is to guide him in using the means he has? Wesley's surprising reply is, Save—and Give.

Save all you can. The poorest can save nothing except at the cost of health, and that is losing, not saving. But, for the rest of us, to save that we may give is our duty.

Save, by avoiding waste and extravagance. The counsel springs out of the conviction that the outward life of a Christian should be simple, unaffected, modest. He is to live for the primary things, and count the trappings of life secondary. ' It is my prayer,' wrote Paul to Philippi, ' that your love may be more and more rich in knowledge and all manner of insight, enabling you to have a sense of what is vital.'[1] It is this sense of what is vital that rules out, with ready content, the unimportant. It lies behind Wesley's statement of the case against thoughtless spending : in food, he says, ' be content with what plain nature requires ' ; in clothing, ' do not waste . . . by superfluous or expensive apparel, or by needless ornaments ' ; in general, ' lay out nothing to gratify the pride of life, to gain the admiration or praise of men.'

Elsewhere, in an incisive passage, he relates the Christian duty of economy to social need : ' let our superfluities give way to our neighbour's conveniences (and who then will have any superfluities left ?) ; our conveniences to our neighbour's necessities ; our necessities to his extremities.'[2]

In the library of Headingley College there is a letter written by Wesley—

---

[1] i. 9 (Moffatt's translation).
[2] Tenth Discourse *Upon our Lord's Sermon on the Mount.*

dated Bristol, September 9, 1776—
which illustrates the harmony between
his practice and his preaching. It is
in reply to a form sent out by the Commissioners of Excise beginning, ' As the
Commissioners cannot doubt but you
have plate for which you have hitherto
neglected to make an entry.' Wesley
replies, ' I have two silver tea-spoons
at London and two at Bristol. This
is all the plate I have at present, and
I shall not buy any more while so many
round me want bread.' Instinctively,
thought turns to One greater than
Wesley, who chose the artisan's home,
the carpenter's trade and the way-
farer's lot, who came not to be served
but to serve, through whose poverty
the race is becoming rich.

We may expand Wesley's Second
Counsel, so as to draw out its social
meaning, thus :

> Save all you can, being con-
> tent with simple wholesome
> ways that you may be ready
> to serve the present age.

Practical questions remain. For example, how ought a parent to provide for his child or children? A son or daughter for aged parents? Any man or woman for any dependent on him or her? The doctrine of Gain—Save —Give meets each case. These of our family circle are our nearest neighbours, for whom responsibility is immediate; that responsibility is to be met, and can be met most readily, where personal habits are not wasteful.

What of provision for the future of one's children and other relatives? Most people have little to bequeath; but to such of his hearers as were wealthy Wesley's convictions led him to offer pungent advice. ' Give each ' —that is, leave to each—' what would keep him above want.' ' If you have good reason to believe they would waste what is now in your possession in gratifying, and thereby increasing, the desire of the flesh, the desire of the eye, or the pride of life, at the peril of theirs, and your own soul, do not set these traps in their way.'

But already we are launched on the discussion of the Third Counsel, *Give all you can.*

'Take, have, and keep are pleasant words,' runs an old English saying. 'Gain, save, and give,' taught Wesley. The difference centres in the third term, and it is the difference between two worlds of thought. Are men to gain and save to keep or to give? Disguise it in what words we may, the answer marks the difference between a niggard and a Christian. 'Every one is covetous whose beneficence does not increase in the same proportion as his substance,' said Wesley.[1]

Here centres what Jesus called 'the deceitfulness of riches,' the subtle power of money to turn men into money-lovers. 'It is no more sinful to be rich than to be poor, but it is dangerous beyond expression,' wrote

[1] Tyerman, *Life and Times of John Wesley*, iii., p. 373.

Wesley in Birmingham in 1788. And still more plainly in an earlier advice to the Methodists : ' This will be their grand danger ; as they are industrious and frugal, they must needs increase in goods. This appears already ; in London, Bristol, and most other trading towns, those who are in business have increased in substance sevenfold, some of them twenty, yea, an hundredfold. What need, then, have these of the strongest warnings, lest they be entangled therein and perish.'[1]

His strong warnings continued. In 1789, two years before his death, he wrote in Dublin : ' Does it not seem (and yet this cannot be) that Christianity, true scriptural Christianity, has a tendency, in process of time, to undermine and destroy itself ? For wherever true Christianity spreads, it must cause diligence and frugality, which, in the natural course of things, must beget riches ! and riches naturally beget pride, love of the world, and

[1] Sermon on *Dives and Lazarus*.

every temper that is destructive of
Christianity. . . . But is there no way
to prevent this ? Allowing that diligence and frugality must produce
riches, is there no means to hinder
riches from destroying the religion of
those that possess them ? I can see
only one possible way ; find out another who can. Do you gain all you
can and save all you can ? Then you
must, in the nature of things, grow
rich. Then if you have any desire
to escape the damnation of hell, give
all you can ; otherwise I can have
no more hope of your salvation than
of that of Judas Iscariot. I call
God to record upon my soul, that I
advise no more than I practise. I do,
blessed be God, gain, and save, and
give all I can.'[1]

His moral authority for this strong
speech was, first, that the counsel,
Give all you can, seemed to him the
only practical way of obeying the
command of Jesus, 'Lay not up for

[1] Sermon on *Causes of the Inefficacy of Christianity.*

yourselves treasures upon the earth ';
his second credential, let it be empha-
sized, was his personal practice.   Wesley was not, as he would have put it,
a good Jew, giving a tenth to God ;
nor a good Pharisee, giving a fifth ;
he was a Christian, and therefore gave
all.   ' The profits on his cheap books
enabled him to give away as much as
£1,400 a year.'[1]   In Mr. Curnock's
words, Wesley ' was an itinerant Poor
Fund, Chapel Fund, Preachers' and
Preachers' Widows' Fund, and family
friend.'   A Miss Lewen bequeathed
him £1,000 : ' I am God's steward for
the poor,' he wrote, and among the
poor it was soon distributed.[2]   A year
before he died, Tyerman tells us, he
closed his cash-book with the following
words, written with a tremulous hand
so as scarcely to be legible, ' For up-
wards of eighty-six years I have kept

[1] Telford, ' John   Wesley ' in   *Encyclopaedia
Britannica*.
[2] Tyerman, *Life and Times of John Wesley*, Vol. ii.,
p. 589.

my accounts exactly; I will not attempt it any longer, being satisfied with the continual conviction that I save all I can, and give all I can; that is, all I have.'[1]

It is imperative to be clear here, even at the risk of repetition. Wesley's teaching, summarized in his own words, is as follows :

' It is allowed (1) That we are to provide necessaries and conveniences for those of our own household; (2) that men in business are to lay up as much as is necessary for the carrying on of that business; (3) that we are to leave our children what will supply them with necessaries and conveniences after we have left the world; and (4) that we are to provide things honest in the sight of all men, so as to ' " owe no man anything." '

' But to lay up any more, when this is done, is what our Lord has flatly forbidden. . . . If, when this is done, there is an overplus left, then do good

[1] Ibid. i. 436.

to them that are of the household of
faith. If there be an overplus still,
" as you have opportunity do good
unto all men." In so doing, you *give
all you can* ; nay, in a sound sense,
all you have. For all that is laid out
in this manner is really given to God.
You render unto God the things that
are God's, not only by what you give
to the poor, but also by what you
expend in providing things needful for
yourself and your household '[1]

We may expand Wesley's Third
Counsel so as to bring within its scope
all these considerations, thus :

> Give all you can, avoiding the
> perils of riches by providing
> honestly for the needs of your-
> self and your household and
> giving all else to meet the needs
> of others.

The new standard of values which
Christ proclaimed, fully acknowledged
and faithfully applied, leads, we have

[1] Sermon on *The Danger of Riches.*

seen, to a new practice in money matters. Wesley's doctrine of *Gain—Save—Give* has this high value as a guide to practice: it accords with the plainest sense of Christ's plainest sayings concerning money. It whittles nothing away. It owns His word as law, and obeys.

The content of the Christian Negative, ' doing no harm,' has now been explored. We proceed to examine the content of the Christian Positive, ' doing good.'

F

CHAPTER IV

A MODERN STUDY OF THE
' RULES '

2. THE CHRISTIAN POSITIVE

Is it not right that all our life should be one continued labour of love? If a day passes without doing good, may not one well say with Titus, ' My friends, I have lost a day.'

JOHN WESLEY,
An Earnest Appeal to Men of Reason and Religion, 1743.

CHAPTER IV

A MODERN STUDY OF THE 'RULES'

2. THE CHRISTIAN POSITIVE

THE statement of the modes of doing good is as arresting as that of the abstinences from evil. It is notable also for a description of the frame of mind and soul of those who would do good of every possible sort to all men.

I

The people called Methodists were to continue to evidence their desire of salvation, the *Rules* go on to say :

SECONDLY, By doing good, by being in every kind merciful after their power ;

as they have opportunity, doing good of
every possible sort, and as far as is possible,
to all men ;

To their bodies, of the ability that God
giveth, by giving food to the hungry,
by clothing the naked, by visiting or
helping them that are sick or in
prison ;

To their souls, by instructing, reproving,
or exhorting all they have any intercourse
with ; trampling under foot that enthusiastic doctrine of devils, that ' we are
not to do good, unless our heart be free
to it.'

By doing good especially to them that are
of the household of faith, or groaning so
to be ; employing them preferably to
others, buying one of another, helping
each other in business ; and so much the
more, because the world will love its own,
and them only.

By all possible diligence and frugality,
that the gospel be not blamed.

By running with patience the race that
is set before them, denying themselves,
and taking up their cross daily ; submitting to bear the reproach of Christ ;
to be as the filth and offscouring of the
world ; and looking that men should say
all manner of evil of them falsely, for the
Lord's sake.

The first generation of Methodists knew nothing of religion divorced from social duties. After the manner of the New Testament they preached salvation by faith only; by the same token they held faith, apart from good works, merely nominal and lifeless. 'We speak of a faith,' said John Wesley, 'productive of good works and all holiness.'[1] He would have accepted Luther's putting of the case: 'a Christian man does not live in himself, but in Christ and in his neighbour, or else is no Christian; in Christ by faith, in his neighbour by love.' Yet to the term 'neighbour' Wesley gave a more consistent interpretation than did Luther, who deserted the peasants of Germany in their need.

Wesley worked out the idea of a 'productive' faith in two spheres. There were duties to every man. There

[1] Sermon on *Salvation by Faith*.

were duties to ' the household of the faith.'

II

The statement of a Christian's duties to every man is, first, a statement of ministries to physical needs. The Methodist was to do good to all men,

> *To their bodies, of the ability that God giveth, by giving food to the hungry, by clothing the naked, by visiting or helping them that are sick or in prison.*

This conception of ' productive ' faith is clearly reminiscent of the Judgement Scene in Matt. xxv. Food and clothing for the needy, fellowship with the sick and the prisoners, are named. But there was neither frontier nor time limit to Wesley's scheme of social service. ' Good of every possible sort, and, as far as is possible, to all men,' is the rich phrase. Or, to

use another fine and frequent word
of his, the true Christian is a ' lover of
mankind.'

> I knew that Christ had given me birth
> To brother all the souls on earth,

he would have shouted with Saul Kane
in joy.

The only bound to service in practical life was ' opportunity ' : ' as they
have opportunity, doing good.' The
range of neighbourly opportunity ex-
tends in each generation. In the
eighteenth century it was much more
circumscribed than to-day. Consider
two examples :

The destitution caused then when
trade was bad, or low wages bred want,
or sickness shattered prosperity, could
only be dealt with by charity and in
individual cases. Neighbour helped
neighbour. A long frost in January,
1740, threw hundreds out of work in
Bristol ; Wesley made collections and
fed the starving. When the Thames

was fast frozen in the winter of 1763
he opened the Foundery, the Methodist
preaching-room, and gave pease pottage
and barley broth to the destitute
watermen and their families. He
established, at various times, a dis-
pensary for the sick poor, a poor-house
for aged widows, a school for untaught
children, and a loan fund for the
advance of small sums of money to
Methodists in distress. Opportunity to
cope with destitution is vastly greater
in the twentieth century. While the
loving personal service of man to
man will never be out of date, an
awakening national conscience now
searches out the causes of poverty and
disease ; and finds additional imple-
ments of succour in the new knowledge
which scientist and economist add to
our store, and in the making and ad-
ministering of law.

So, also, in some degree, with war
and its horrors. What could the
eighteenth-century follower of Him who
said ' Blessed are the peacemakers '

do when war raged with France, save preach in camp like John Haime in Flanders, or comfort the widow and fatherless at home, or visit the French prisoners as Wesley did at Bristol and raise funds to clothe their nakedness? To-day, democracy's deepening hatred of war, and the growing power of public influence to hold in check the feuds of courts and parties, point to a rapidly widening field of influence for the lover of peace.

The modern disciple of Jesus is a citizen of the whole world. It is literally true that a man to-day can do good ' to all men.' The hungry in India are within his reach ; the oppressed in Africa not beyond his protection. His ' chance of noble deeds ' covers wide possibilities of public influence and service, as well as time-honoured ways of neighbourly love. To serve the present age effectively disciples of Jesus need to use its new opportunities to the full, as the men of the eighteenth century used the more limited opportunities of their time. The new instruments of social succour, furnished to-day by city and by State, are tools for Christian hands.

What of responsibility for the souls of all men ? The second statement of the Christian's duty to every man is a statement of ministries to the spiritual needs of his neighbour. The Methodist people were to do good to the souls of all,

> *By instructing, reproving, or ex-*
> *horting all they have any inter-*
> *course with ; trampling under foot*
> *that enthusiastic doctrine of devils,*
> *that we ' are not to do good, unless*
> *our heart be free to it.'*

Mr. Birrell, in his picturesque way, compares Wesley's untiring evangelism to electioneering. John Wesley, he says, ' contested the three kingdoms in the cause of Christ during a campaign which lasted forty years.' It is a vivid and truthful picture. To listen to Wesley claiming the suffrages of Britain for Jesus is to hear a man aflame with passion for souls. Take the final appeal of his Sermon on *Justification by Faith* : ' Who art thou,' he cries, ' that now seest and feelest both thine inward and outward ungodliness ? Thou art the man ! I want thee for my Lord ! I challenge *thee* for a child of God by faith ! The Lord hath need of thee. Thou who feelest thou art just fit for hell, art just fit to advance His glory ; the glory of His free grace, justifying the ungodly and him that worketh not. O come quickly ! Believe in the Lord Jesus, and thou, even thou, art reconciled to God.'

Read that passion into the words of the *Rules*, and the secret of this pristine zeal is laid bare. From parent to child, workman to workman, preacher to hearer, the message ran : ' I want thee for my Lord ! ' England, Scotland, Ireland, and Wales, and America too, must own the supremacy of

Jesus. Charles Wesley taught his congregations to sing of grace for every man :

> Lovers of pleasure more than God,
>   For you He suffered pain ;
> Swearers, for you He spilt His blood ;
>   And shall He bleed in vain ?
>
> Misers, for you His life He paid,
>   Your basest crime He bore ;
> Drunkards, your sins on Him are laid,
>   That you might sin no more.

So the word went out to all, to the careless and the callous, for had not Jesus died for all ?

Horace Walpole wrote satirically in 1749, ' The Methodists love your big sinners, as proper subjects to work upon ; and, indeed, they have a plentiful harvest.' Wesley went harvesting all the year round. The Quietist, an easy-going labourer, pressed his view again and again on him : ' We are not to do good unless our heart be free to it.' Once Wesley purposefully tried the plan. He was

riding from London to Markfield beyond Leicester, a two-days' journey by
chaise, and this is his record : ' For
these two days I had made an experi-
ment which I had been so often and
earnestly pressed to do ; speaking to
none concerning the things of God,
unless my heart was free to it. And
what was the event ? Why (1) That
I spoke to none at all for four-score
miles together ; no, not even to him
that travelled with me in the chaise,
unless a few words at first setting out.
(2) That I had no cross either to bear
or to take up, and commonly in an
hour or two fell fast asleep. (3) That
I had much respect shown me wherever
I came ; every one behaving to me as to
a civil, good-natured gentleman. Oh,
how pleasing is all this to flesh and
blood ! Need ye " compass sea and
land " to make " proselytes " to this ? '

It was a cheap and easy avoidance
of the cross of the Christian confessor,
in Wesley's judgement, and therefore
a ' doctrine of devils ' to be trampled

under foot. In a burning sentence
he withers up the plea of the Quietist :
' The lover of mankind has no eye at
all to his own temporal advantage . . .
for while he is on the full stretch to
save their souls from death, he, as it
were, forgets himself.' [1]

*On the full stretch to save their souls
from death.* How much do we—God
forgive us !—know of that passion ?
There is an unfearing testimony to
truth, a frank declaration of faith in
the unseen, a willing witness to the
reality of spiritual experiences, an
urgent appeal for the acceptance of
Christ as Saviour, each of which life
to-day most certainly is claiming from
us.

III

The other sphere for ' productive '
faith was the household of the faithful.

---

[1] Second Discourse *Upon our Lord's Sermon on
the Mount.*

' I shall endeavour to show,' says Wesley in his Fourth Discourse *Upon the Sermon on the Mount,* ' that Christianity is essentially a social religion ; and that to turn it into a solitary one is to destroy it.' It was because Christianity was essentially social, and a solitary Christian ' little less than a contradiction in terms,' that the Methodist people were charged to be servants of humanity, in every kind merciful after their power to the bodies and souls of all men.

Yet humanity is a vast circle whose circumference the men of that age could only imagine. Right at hand were brothers in need, members of an inner circle in which fellowship, practical as well as mystical, should rule. The Pauline counsel, rich in sacramental association, and the quarry from which Wesley gathered the great words of his Christian Positive, ran : ' As we have therefore opportunity let us do good unto all men, *especially unto them who are of the household of the faith.*' Next

G

the statement of the Christian Nega
tive.

The exposition of the Christian
Negative, ' doing no harm,' worked
inwards, so to say, from the surface
of life to its core. Sins on the ' black
list ' of that day were first repudiated
Then breaches of the Golden Rule no
commonly confessed as evil were placed
under the Christian ban. The central
rottenness of a life careless or contemp
tuous of others' rights was last of al
laid bare ; out of the heart, as Jesus
said, come forth evil thoughts and
deeds ; therefore a self-considering
money-loving, habit of mind was dis
closed as the source of the evils most
generally practised.

On a parallel line of thought the
exposition of the Christian Positive
' doing good,' reaches its final ex
pression. True Christian faith is pro
ductive of good works. A Christian
in earnest will be the helper of every
man ; he cannot but be touched with
the feeling of our common infirmities

overty and sickness and grief, and
he inner shame and burden of sin.
Especially will he be a Greatheart in
he Christian pilgrim company, saying
y his doing, ' Let them that are
most afraid keep close to me.' But
what manner of spirit, what turn of
mind, will make possible this daily
ractice of doing good ?

That is the question to which the
losing sentences of the second section
f the *Rules* give this answer. An ease-
oving, self-indulging habit of mind
ings off social responsibilities, light-
earted and uncaring ; only a dis-
iplined and sacrificial habit of mind
ill shoulder them cheerfully and con-
antly. So the *Rules* require all who
ontinue in the Societies to do good

By all possible diligence and fru-
gality, that the gospel be not blamed.
By running with patience the race
that is set before them, denying
themselves, and taking up their
cross daily, submitting to bear the

reproach of Christ; to be as the
filth and offscouring of the world
and looking that men should say
all manner of evil of them falsely
for the Lord's sake.

The terms are strong, and so of
necessity. God calls for unusual obediences in an age of swift and world-
wide change ; that is the truth common
to the eighteenth and twentieth centuries. Christians in earnest must
adapt their lives to the urgency of God's
call. 'My meat is to do the will of
Him that sent Me, and to accomplish
His work,' said the Teacher : dare the
disciple be other than diligent ? 'The
Son of Man hath not where to lay His
head ' : ought His follower to be other
than frugal and self-spending ? The
gospel will certainly be blamed if
Christ's way of life and the Christian's
diverge.

John Wesley had moral right to
impress *diligence* on the character of
the Methodist.

' Leisure and I have taken leave
of one another,' he wrote his brother
Samuel ; ' I propose to be busy as long
as I live if my health is so long indulged
me.' That was in his twenty-third
year. ' Idleness slays,' is Mr. Curnock's reading of a cipher entry, of
about the same date, in Wesley's
diary. Sixty-four years later, on New
Year's Day, 1790, he penned in his
diary, ' I am now an old man . . .
however, blessed be God, *I do not slack
my labour.'* Practice and precept
travelled together. That gave power
to a saying such as this, flung out to
the undergraduates of Oxford from the
pulpit of St. Mary's : ' Do you redeem
the time, crowding as much work into
every day as it can contain ? ' That
also gave point to his word, ' A Christian abhors sloth as much as drunkenness ; and flees from idleness as he does
from adultery.'[1] An easy, indolent,
fashionable life is, he held with truth,

[1] Ninth Discourse *Upon our Lord's Sermon on the
Mount*

legitimate only to one who is ' a
stranger to this whole affair ' of
Christianity. To one of his preachers
in Ireland, whose slack ways distressed
him, Wesley wrote, ' Be active, be
diligent ; avoid all laziness, sloth,
indolence. Fly from every degree,
every appearance of it ; else you
will never be more than half a
Christian.'

It has already been shown that with
equal moral right he urged *frugality*.
The point deserves further illustra-
tion.

There is a sentence in the *Quaker
Book of Discipline* which fully expresses
his view of Christian duty in this
respect : ' It is peculiarly necessary in
the age in which we live that the
Christian man and woman should
observe simplicity and moderation in
their manners and dress, in the furniture of their houses, in their style of
living.' The Fourth Discourse *Upon
our Lord's Sermon on the Mount* concludes with words singularly akin.

Says Wesley, ' In order to enlarge your
ability of doing good, renounce all
superfluities. Cut off all unnecessary
expense in food, in furniture, in
apparel. Be a steward of every gift
of God, even of these His lowest gifts.
Cut off all unnecessary expense of time,
all needless or useless employments ;
and " whatsoever thy hand findeth
to do, do it with thy might." '

By this standard he lived. ' What
gain did I seek among you ? ' he asks
of his contemporaries at Oxford, his
Lincoln parishioners, his American congregations, and his British Societies.
' Food and raiment I have ; such food
as I choose to eat, and such raiment
as I choose to put on. I have a place
where to lay my head. I have what is
needful for life and godliness. And
I apprehend this is all the world can
afford. The kings of the earth can
give me no more. For as to gold and
silver, I count it dung and dross. . . .
I desire it not ; I seek it not. . . It
must indeed pass through my hands

but I will take care (God being my helper) that the mammon of unrighteousness shall only pass through ; it shall not rest there.'[1]

In this faith he died. ' I particularly desire,' he laid it down in his will, ' there may be no hearse, no coach, no escutcheon, no pomp. . . . I solemnly adjure my executors, in the name of God, punctually to observe this.'

The poverty of his father's lot, as a country parson in Lincolnshire, may have taught him thrift. But Christian frugality, as Wesley conceived it, is a higher and costlier virtue than thrift ; for thrift, as some practise it, is no virtue at all, but selfishness misnamed. Christian frugality saves to spend. It saves by avoidance of needless expenditure on personal comfort ; it spends freely and joyously on others' needs. That makes it *Christian* frugality, the antithesis alike of meanness and extravagance.

[1] *An Earnest Appeal to Men of Reason and Religion.*

' See that poor member of Christ,'
Wesley exclaims, ' pinched with hunger, shivering with cold, half naked !
Meantime you have plenty of this
world's goods—of meat, drink, and
apparel. In the name of God, what
are you doing ? Do you neither fear
God, nor regard man ? Why do you
not deal your bread to the hungry, and
cover the naked with a garment ?
Have you laid out in your own costly
apparel what would have answered
both these intentions ? Did God command you so to do ? Does He com-
mend you for so doing ? You well
know He does not. This idle expense
has no approbation, either from God
or your own conscience. But you say
you can *afford* it ! Oh, be ashamed to
take such miserable nonsense into
your mouths ! Never more utter such
stupid cant ; such palpable absurdity !
Can any servant *afford* to lay out his
Master's money, any otherwise than
his Master appoints him ? So far
from it, that whoever does this ought

to be excluded from a Christian
society.'[1]

Each added statement of the Christian's duty emphasizes the divergence
of his Rule of Life from the conventional type of living. There is sever-
ance in method and aim, in method
because of aim. To run with patience
the race set before us ; to deny ourselves ; to take up our cross daily ; to
bear the reproach of Christ ; to be as
the filth and off-scouring of the world ;
to look that men should say all manner
of evil of us falsely, for the Lord's sake :
what is the heart, the innermost meaning, of these phrases so fruitlessly
familiar to us ? This. That for the
ventures of the Kingdom of Heaven we
are to order and, if need be, surrender
life, Jesus, in the days of His flesh,
being our Pattern.

Men who ignore the Christian obligation sacrifice to themselves. We have
an altar, and a sacrifice—ourselves.
The cross, in modern speech, is the

[1] Sermon on *Causes of the Inefficacy of Christianity.*

pouring-out of life for the life of the whole world. To bear the cross of the Christian confessor is to be burdened daily, to bleed in spirit daily, for human sin and wrong. In a sense which experience only can explain, the warfare of the Kingdom is a fellowship of the sufferings of the Christ. Life, and life alone, can fill the empty vessel of the world's need. The claims of social justice, and the call of the nations to the Church of the Saviour, are not to be met by acquiescences and alms. They can only be adequately answered by the self-giving of living, loving men and women.

To drink the cup of a Saviour, to be baptized with His baptism, is to be ready to follow to Gethsemane and Golgotha. 'All things are cleansed with blood, and apart from shedding of blood there is no remission.' Of Sir John Franklin and his fellow discoverers who perished in the Arctic wastes, in the finding of the North-West passage, it is written, ' They

forged the last link with their lives.'
On no other terms can the chain of
Christ's world-conquests be made com-
plete

CHAPTER V

A MODERN STUDY OF THE 'RULES'

3. THE SECRET OF THE CHRISTIAN DYNAMIC

As flowers their opening leaves display,
  And glad drink in the solar fire,
So may we catch Thy every ray,
  So may Thy influence us inspire;
Thou Beam of the eternal Beam,
  Thou purging Fire, Thou quickening Flame.
                    GERHARD TERSTEEGEN
                    (John Wesley's Translation).

CHAPTER V

A MODERN STUDY OF THE 'RULES'

3. THE SECRET OF THE CHRISTIAN DYNAMIC

I

WHO is sufficient for all these things?

To do no harm and especially to turn resolutely from the evil most generally practised ; to do good of every possible sort, and, as far as possible, to all men ; to sustain these high resolves through dreary days and in unsympathetic company ; in the whole of life to move 'straight toward God, and that continually, walking steadily on in the highway of holiness, in the paths of justice, mercy, and truth ' : this is a prodigious task, since we are men, not angels.

Nevertheless, the first recruits to the standard of the risen Jesus were in no doubt about the feasibility of the undertaking. They were actually known as the people of ' the Way,'[1]— that is, as men and women who held to a singular mode of living, anti-conventional rather than unconventional.

Nor was Wesley in any doubt on this vital matter. The Christian Rule of Life had been recovered, and it could be obeyed. The New Testament ' Way ' was one which plain folk could follow, for God's wisdom would aid their wits. ' It is no small thing,' he says, ' to lay out for God all which you have received from God. It requires all your wisdom, all your resolution, all your patience and constancy—far more than ever you had by nature, but not more than you may have by grace. For His grace is

[1] See Acts ix. 2, xix. 9, 23, xxii. 4, xxiv. 14, 22, in the Revised Version.

sufficient for you ; and all things, you know, are possible to him that believeth.'[1] The Christian Negative, doing no harm, and the Christian Positive, doing good, become practical politics to those who know the secret of the Christian Dynamic.

The final section of the *Rules* points the way to this secret. ' It is expected of all who desire to continue in these (Methodist) Societies,' so run the terms of the disclosure, ' that they should continue to evidence their desire of salvation,'

THIRDLY, By attending upon all the ordinances of GOD ; such are,
The public worship of God ;
The ministry of the word, either read or expounded ;
The Supper of the Lord ;
Family and private prayer ;
Searching the Scriptures ; and
Fasting or abstinence.

The Wesleys never suggested **that**

[1] Sermon on *The Good Steward.*

these ordinances of God were in themselves the Christian Dynamic. Their
teaching stoutly opposed so mechanical
a view. The Christian Dynamic is
contact with Christ. But the value of
the ordinances, as divinely appointed
'means,' is that in them the questful
spirit of man meets, as by tryst, the
Spirit of Jesus who empowers. A
commanding instance is that of the
earliest company of Christian believers.
The record runs of them that
'they devoted themselves to the in-
struction given by the apostles and to
fellowship, breaking bread and praying
together.'[1] These were the men and
women whose daring divergence from
accepted ideas of right and wrong
earned for them the sobriquet, 'the
Way.' Their moral energy and power
of endurance were sustained in this
rapturous discipline of the soul; for
to attend in devoutness of spirit upon
all the ordinances of God is to build

[1] Acts ii. 42.

up reserves of strength and to school the soul for service.

II

The case for the construction and observance of a discipline of the devout life needs to be stated with care ; since it is not a bare, still less a hollow, regard for sacred times and seasons which is of worth.

'Temple-treading' and hypocrisy have gone together before, and will again. Wesley sharply and frequently distinguished between 'the men of outside religion' and those who bore 'the marks of the new birth.' 'Go to church twice a day ; go to the Lord's table every week ; say ever so many prayers in private ; hear ever so many good sermons ; read ever so many good books ; still "you must be born again" : none of these things will stand in the place of the new birth ; no, nor any other thing under heaven.'[1] The

[1] Sermon on *The New Birth*.

means of grace could not take the place of everyday goodness ; to use them ' as a kind of commutation for the religion they were designed to subserve ' was to ' turn God's arms against Himself.' [1]

Always the test question must be, ' *To what purpose* is the multitude of your sacrifices unto Me ? ' One of the earliest of Charles Wesley's hymns expresses this inward debate. It contrasts formalism and realism in worship. The Formalist makes his confession :

> Oft did I with the assembly join,
> And near Thine altar drew ;
> A form of godliness was mine,
> The power I never knew.

But formalism must yield when the soul's real needs surge upward. In all his care for ' the means ' the Formalist had

> The spirit in the letter lost,
> The substance in the shade.

[1] Sermon on *The Means of Grace*.

And so at last reality speaks. Only Christ can satisfy the Realist in the realm of the spirit.

> Jesus, to Thee my soul looks up,
> 'Tis Thou must make it new.

Once a man has discerned that, then each ' means ' becomes to him ' a means of *grace*,' a new revealing of the Presence of his Saviour. The Formalist becomes the Realist, and can sing :

> Still for Thy lovingkindness, Lord,
> I in Thy temple wait ;
> I look to find *Thee* in Thy word,
> Or at Thy table meet.

Such attendance upon all the ordinances of God is not formal, but of faith. It is the renewal of fealty to Christ. It will sometimes mark a fresh stage in the search for truth or in the will to venture all for the Kingdom.

This is but another way of saying that the means of grace are a quest of the Lord of grace and a fellowship with Him.

> Here, in Thine own appointed ways,
>   I wait to learn Thy will

is the voice of the Christian Realist. In the public worship of God the hope and faith of such a disciple is to meet the Mediator between God and man, Himself man Christ Jesus; in the ministry of the word he looks for a new vision of his Redeemer; at the Supper of the Lord he waits to discern the Real Presence of the Saviour; in family and private prayer, weary and heavy laden or light of heart and hopeful, he makes response to Him who said, ' Come unto Me '; in searching the Scriptures he sits at the feet of the supreme Teacher; in fasting or abstinence aspires to learn the will of Jesus. The ordinances of God, to such a worshipper, are means to apprehend his ' sole liege and Lord, Jesus Christ.'

Apart from Christ the ordinances are mere frames for devotion, machinery without motive-power ; but to meet Him in the ordinances is to make contact with the Christian Dynamic. It is to know certainly that the Christian Rule of Life is practicable to-day, despite the perplexing intricacies of commerce and custom. Because Jesus lives, because the Spirit of Jesus can sway the spirit of man, because the self-same Spirit can subdue the rebel in our soul and in the soul of the race, all things that make for righteousness are possible. The Pauline experience can be the experience of the Christian adventurer in modern Britain : ' I have been initiated into the secret of all sorts and conditions of life, for plenty and for hunger, for prosperity and for privations. In Him who strengthens me I am able for anything.'[1]

---

[1] Phil. iv. 12–13 (Moffatt's translation).

III

In another respect the case for the construction and observance of a discipline of the devout life needs careful statement. ' Why,' some will say, ' speak of order and discipline in the spiritual life ? Let well alone. We were redeemed by love, the love of God ; we should live by love, and love needs no rules.'

Without questioning that there are natures blithely innocent of any need of the conscious shaping of modes of spiritual devotion, still less denying that love, untrammelled and unforced, is the mainspring of Christian duty, there are three reasons why to many the building up of habits of meditation and prayer is of incalculable worth. First, their quality as Christians is poorer without these. Again, the Christian Rule of Life is so dramatically opposed to the conventional way of living that they continually require spiritual reinforcement. Finally, a

long line of religious experience,
including that of our Redeemer,
attests the value of *habits* of worship,
individual and corporate.

The first two reasons are personal.
' It plainly appears,' says John Wesley,
whose diaries show with what precision
he attended the means of grace, that
' God does not continue to act upon the
soul, unless the soul reacts upon God.' [1]
But under the stress of modern life
the rights and duties of the soul are
easily forgotten. With one, the cause
is the strain of business ; with another,
the exacting claims of public affairs ;
with a third, the engrossing visible
concerns of the Church, its organiza-
tions and assemblies ; with a fourth,
family cares. It is a standing diffi-
culty with earnest men and women
in this hustling age to define their
sphere of legitimate duty. Here is one
guide-post. The legitimate becomes
the illegitimate when it denies to the

[1] Sermon upon *The Great Privilege of Those that
are Born of God.*

soul its rights. The first right of the soul is seclusion, space and time for communion with the Eternal One, the Father of spirits. If seclusion involves exclusion, the Christian must exclude. Life's time-table must be recast to find due place for the ordinances of God.

This is not selfishness; it is unworldly wisdom. It is not artificial, but sacrificial. Unaided man simply cannot avoid evil in every kind and do good of every possible sort. Yet these are the paramount duties of the soul, the outward Rule of Life for the modern disciple of Jesus. But the soul, like the body, is unable to discharge its duties unless its rights are respected. The life of the soul must be vigorous or it cannot work vigorously. Moral expenditure is dependent upon spiritual income. Time to ' react upon God ' is therefore necessary for humanity's sake.

The supreme proof is the example of Jesus. His life in Palestine shows that worship of the Father is vital to a sacrificial career, and, because vital, cannot be restricted to public occasions, but must in addition seek and shape personal and private forms.

The student of the life of Jesus can recognize three provinces of spiritual communion entered by Him.

He joined habitually in the public worship of Jehovah. Luke's record of the return to Nazareth is that Jesus ' entered, *as His custom was*, into the synagogue on the sabbath day.' He was present at the annual religious festivals of the Jews ; the great Feasts are indissolubly linked with great passages in His teaching and momentous happenings of His ministry.

He also created a closer fellowship with kindred souls. The Twelve were called ' that they might be with Him,' comrades as well as learners. With them He communed of the nature and ways of the Father, of the Hebrew Scripture, of prayer and its potency, and of things concerning the Kingdom

of God.   With them and for them He
prayed.

One shrinks from words in thinking
of the innermost shrine of the devotion
of Jesus.   It is sacred beyond speech.
Let one citation from the Gospel
according to Luke stand without comment.   It records the retreat for prayer
before the choice of the men to whom,
after training and test, the crusade
for the Kingdom should be committed :

> ' He went out into the moun-
> tain to pray ; *and He continued
> all night in prayer to God.* And
> when it was day, He called His
> disciples : and He chose from
> them twelve, whom also He
> named apostles.'

What is the discipline of the devout
life which the modern disciple of Jesus
may keep as his inward Rule ?

It is most surely based on the practice of Jesus.   Wesley's statement of
Christian obligation covers the same

area, and the same three provinces of spiritual communion are marked in his thought. These are, the public acts of divine worship; the more intimate fellowships of the Christian company; and the creation of habits of private devotion.

IV

The Public Acts of Divine Worship

The first of the three provinces of spiritual communion includes two of the ordinances of God upon which the *Rules* require the Methodist to attend :

> *The public worship of God :*
> *The ministry of the word, either read*
> *or expounded.*

The two are ordinarily one in the custom of the Church.

The public worship of God implies an appointed day for public worship.

This raises at once the question of the religious use of Sunday. It is urgent. Not by hostile argument but by indifferent actions it has come to pass that the historic religious associations of the Lord's Day are ignored by multitudes.

What is the duty of the Christian in respect of Sunday? He must assert and exercise the rights of the soul. Here is part of his distinctive witness to the age, a witness against the mood and movement of the age. Love of money increases the area of Sunday trading : to the instructed Christian money is servant, not master, and may not trespass where spiritual duties have authority. Love of pleasure dedicates the Day to the cult of physical health, reviving unawares the solitary belief of second-century paganism in Aesculapius, the god of bodily health, and calling him *Sōtēr*, Saviour : Christianity honours the body by exalting the soul and training the kingly element in man for kingship. No informed disciple of Jesus who loved the lilies of the field can be insensible to the wonder of flower or forest ; this is the Father's handiwork, a confession of His goodness and wisdom, ' written with a sunbeam in the great book of the creature,' as Jeremy Taylor finely says ; but thoughtlessly to turn from the assembly of worshippers of God for highway or hedgerow is to drift from the direct quest for the Divine Will, and to sever one's self from the fellowship of Christian prayer and purpose. Against the greed for gain, against the heedless pursuit of pleasure, against the unthinking yet perilous breach with old-time habits of public worship on the Lord's Day, the Christian is to stand.

He is to be a worshipper, not a wanderer, for the sake of the supremacy of the soul. If ' from *within* proceeds a nation's health,' the setting-apart of one day of the week for reflection and divine worship accords with man's highest aspiration. To Christian men

I

and women who have heard in the moral challenge of their times a call of God, the matter is beyond uncertainty ; a zeal for the Holy Day burns with their passion for the Holy City.

Nor is attendance upon the public worship of God to be dependent on the ability of the preacher. The conspicuous place of the sermon in the Order of Service in many Protestant Churches may tend to make men hearers more than worshippers. A renascence of the spirit of reverent adoration of God, Father, Son, and Holy Spirit, is needed, and a recognition that in all honest speaking in His Name Christ Himself speaks. The Day is His enduring memorial, the remembrance through long centuries of His triumph over sin and death, of His gift to the Church of the Spirit, the Helper. In hymn and prayer, in the Scripture and its sincere exposition, Christ ' in whom are all the treasures of wisdom and knowledge hidden ' may be discerned. But the vision is

to the lover of Jesus, not to the critic,
nor to the cynic. This does not lessen
the preacher's responsibility ; he must
account to the highest tribunal ; to his
own Master he standeth or falleth.
Nor is it to say that the dull mind is
the most religious ; rather, that sensi-
tiveness of the presence of Christ
depends upon sympathy. He is not
far from each one of us ; they find Him
who feel after Him. ' I could taste the
good word of God in the anthem,'
wrote Wesley of a service at St. Paul's,
and that was a sufficient test.

So the true counsel for the Christian
hearer is that he be first and in all a
worshipper. To cite Jeremy Taylor
again, in *Holy Living* :

' When the word of God is read or
preached to you, be sure you be of a
ready heart and mind, free from worldly
cares and thoughts, diligent to hear,
careful to mark, studious to remember,
and desirous to practise all that is
commanded, and to live according to it ;
do not hear for any other end but to

become better in your life, and to be
instructed in every good work, and to
increase in the love and service of God.'

To hear to that end on the first day of
the week will go far to make each day
of the week a Lord's Day.

Of the family and neighbourly duties
between and after the solemnities of
the Day, and of one's social responsibility to assure to others as far as
possible like privileges of worship, it is
enough to say that Christian love should
point the way and Christian wisdom
tread it.

V

The Inner Fellowships of the Church

Of the more intimate fellowships of
the Church Wesley mentions here

The Supper of the Lord

alone.   It should be recalled, however,
that the Methodist Societies were
already grouped in Classes meeting

weekly for spiritual fellowship. The members of a Class were encouraged to speak of their experience as they strove to obey the Christian Rule ; in the Leader was vested the responsibility wisely ' to advise, reprove, comfort, or exhort, as occasion may require.' Co-operation in Christian discipleship was and is the real purpose of the Methodist Class-meeting. Its most characteristic hymn, then and now, sings,

All praise to our redeeming Lord,
    Who joins us by His grace,
And bids us, each to each restored,
    Together seek His face.

He bids us build each other up ;
    And, gathered into one,
To our high calling's glorious hope
    We hand in hand go on.

Hand in hand—that was the primitive Methodist conception of the Christian pilgrim's progress. Hence the peculiar institution of the weekly Class-meeting

as a means of ' social grace.' Hence,
also, Wesley's insistence that the
Methodist people—who, it was assumed,
would attend Class—should be present
at the Supper of the Lord constantly.
For the Eucharist is the chief and
central expression in the Church of
oneness, the oneness of Christians with
Christ as the Body and the Head are
one, the oneness of Christian people as
all are members of the one Body.

The impress of this teaching on early
Methodism was clear and firm. Again
and again Methodists were repelled by
the Anglican clergy from the Lord's
Table simply because they were Methodists, yet Wesley's emphasis on the
duty of communicating regularly did
not change. His pen was busy with
argument and injunction, and the
furnishing of aids to a reverential
observance. He wrote and published
a sermon on *The Duty of Constant
Communion*, and issued broadcast
eucharistic extracts from à Kempis
under the title, *A Companion for the*

Altar. A Collection of Hymns on the Lord's Supper, by John and Charles Wesley, wedded sacred song to solemn rite. In these ways the vital worth of constant communion was taught in cogent terms to those who were to be picked soldiers in the new campaigns of Christ.

The Captain of their salvation, and ours, said, ' This do in remembrance of Me ' ; the soldier's duty is to obey.

Yet no formal obedience avails here. To eat this bread and drink this cup is to proclaim the Captain's dying, its manner and marvel. Greater love had no man than this, for He died for His enemies to make them His friends. He slew enmity by death. To show forth His death after this pattern is to declare the rightful fashion of our life. To follow this Captain in the fight is to fall fighting. ' Love's strength standeth in love's sacrifice ' ; to love as the Captain loved is to give—all. It is this that the symbols of the Lord's death declare, an obedience that falters not

in living or in dying, a broken Body,
outpoured Blood.   In the *Companion
for the Altar* à Kempis represents the
voice of the Beloved, the Saviour, saying to the disciple,

> ' If thou abidest in thyself, and dost
> not offer thyself up freely unto My
> will, thy oblation is not entire,
> neither will the union between
> us be perfect. . . .
> ' So few become *inwardly* free,
> because they cannot wholly deny
> themselves.
> ' My saying is unalterable, *Unless
> a man forsake all, he cannot be My
> disciple !*
> ' Therefore, if thou desirest to be My
> disciple, offer up thyself unto Me
> with thy whole affection.'

The Holy Supper is therefore a
memorial and standard of sacrificial
living and dying.   And more, far
more.   The memorial becomes a communion.   It is a veritable discerning

of Him who fought and fell and rose again. The Captain is there and speaks. The Holy Supper is not an hour of vigil but a place of tryst, a meeting face to face; Captain with follower, the Beloved with the disciple, the Redeemer with the redeemed. With Charles Wesley we too can sing,

> We need not now go up to heaven,
>   To bring the long-sought Saviour down;
> Thou art to all already given,
>   Thou dost even now Thy banquet crown :
> To every faithful soul appear,
> And show Thy real presence here.

They who in faith discern the Real Presence of the Saviour at His appointed place of tryst experience real renewal of soul. To eat the bread, to drink the wine, in loyal allegiance to Christ is to receive Him spiritually. Therein lies the joy of constant communion. To fight the good fight without fear of flinching, a man needs his Captain's unconquerable spirit; and to feed on Him in the heart by faith with thanksgiving is to receive it. This mystic fellowship with Him who was wounded for a world's transgressions can make faltering men strong in travail of soul and carrying of sorrows. Partakers of His most blessed Body and Blood, they partake of His undeviating devotion to the Father's righteous will.

This mystic fellowship with Christ is real, bringing strength. It is also social, bringing spiritual companionship. For the Church, visible and invisible, is indivisible. At the Lord's Table, in sight of the tokens of the death which brings life to each generation, we of one place and age may have fellowship with loyal Christian hearts of every place and age ; with Paul and Polycarp, Augustine and Anselm, Wyclif and Luther and Knox, Bunyan and Wesley, pioneers of the Faith today in India and Africa and otherwhere, disciples of the Saviour who toil in mill and mine, in factory and forest, on rail or shipboard. The Church of the One Foundation is one. Death cannot part nor distance sever the friends of Jesus.

> One army of the living God,
>   To His command we bow;
> Part of His host have crossed the flood,
>   And part are crossing now.

At the feast of remembrance the soldier from the Kingdom's loneliest outpost may lose the sense of his loneliness at the thought of comrades-in-arms; for this Sacrament is Christ our Captain's remembrancer that we are very members incorporate in His mystical body 'which is the blessed company of all faithful people.'

Yet the higher the worth of constant communion the greater the Christian sense of unworthiness of fellowship such as this. We are shamed by so near approach to Christ. The very elements shame us. They betoken Calvary; is there a cross in our heart that answers to His? a pouring out of the soul unto death that others may live?

Small wonder that self-condemned, smitten of conscience, men hold back from communicating, feeling the conflict of impulse which made Keble write,

> It is my Maker—dare I stay?
> My Saviour—dare I turn away?

Is it right to refrain from the Communion because of unworthiness? Because of rank insincerity, yes; but because of unworthiness, assuredly no. He whose property is always to have mercy said, 'Do this.' The Lord's Table is spread for forgiveness, for it is the Table of the Lord, the Redeemer. The Christian penitent and the Christian confessor both have right of place there.

> This eucharistic feast
> *Our every want* supplies.

That was the emphatic teaching of the Wesleys. 'I showed at large,'

wrote John of a day in London in 1740,
' that the persons for whom the Lord's
Supper was ordained are all those who
know and feel that they want the
grace of God, either to restrain them
from sin, or to show their sins forgiven,
or to renew their souls in the image of
God.'

Only the hypocrite does not know
and feel a want of the grace of God.
The honest-hearted Christian, be his
faith feeble or fervent, knows lack and
longing. And the true gospel in the
sacrament is this : ' He that is athirst,
let him come.' Thus to come, truly
and earnestly repentant of sin, seeking
new touch of love with Christ and
neighbour, intending to walk hence-
forth in the holy way, is to make each
Sacramental feast a *sacramentum*, a
new-spoken oath of allegiance to the
Captain of Salvation. It is, to use
the terms of our present thought, an
access to the Christian Dynamic, assur-
ing power to express in workaday life
the Christian Negative, doing no harm,

and the Christian Positive, doing good.

Let the wise, quaint words of Jeremy Taylor, from whom Wesley learned many things, add the final answer. ' All Christian people must come' to the Supper of the Lord, he says. ' They indeed that are in the state of sin must not come so, but yet they must come. First they must quit their state of death, and then partake of the bread of life. They that are at enmity with their neighbours must come—that is no excuse for their not coming ; only they must not bring their enmity along with them, but leave it, and then come. They that have variety of secular employment must come ; only they must leave their secular thoughts and affections behind them, and then come and converse with God. If any man be well grown in grace he must needs come, because he is excellently disposed to so holy a feast : but he that is but in the infancy of piety had need to come that so he may grow in grace.

The strong must come lest they become weak; and the weak that they may become strong. The sick must come to be cured, the healthful to be preserved They that have leisure must come, because they have no excuse; they that have no leisure must come hither, that by so excellent religion they may sanctify their business. The penitent sinners must come, that they may be justified; and they that are justified, that they may be justified still. They that have fears and great reverence to these mysteries, and think no preparation to be sufficient, must receive, that they may learn how to receive the more worthily; and they that have a less degree of reverence must come often to have it heightened: that as those creatures that live amongst the snows of the mountains turn white with their food and conversation with such perpetual whiteness, so our souls may be transformed into the similitude and union with Christ by our perpetual feeding on Him, and conversation, not only in His courts, but in His very heart, and most secret affections, and incomparable purities.'

VI

The Creation of Habits of Private Devotion

The third province of spiritual communion comprises the three ordinances of God which Wesley mentions last in the *Rules* :

> *Family and private prayer;*
> *Searching the Scriptures;*
> *Fasting or abstinence.*

We reach the innermost shrine of worship, the individual and private communion of the disciple with his Lord. Whoso enters here and claims that habit and method should rule must have commanding reasons. For what right has one man to enter the sanctuary of another's life, and seek to order its affairs? To claim a due and reverent observance of the Lord's Day accords with Christian judgement. To emphasize the eucharistic saying of Jesus, ' This do in remembrance of Me,' and to open its hidden wealth, is to urge obligation and privilege. But to lift the veil behind which the soul communes with Christ is to trespass grievously, unless there is an entire justification. Is there?

Bring the issue to a plain and immediate test. ' Enter into thine inner chamber, and having shut thy door, pray to thy Father which is in secret,' said Jesus to His first disciple-company. Again—and this to hostile critics—' Ye search the scriptures . . . and these are they which bear witness of Me.' In last week's life, let us ask, what time was given each day to lonely prayer and the Bible? The honest reply is that with numbers of us prayer is casual, hurried, crowded in or out; while exploration of the Bible is left to the preacher. Where these things are so, do *habits* of private devotion

K

exist, in any sense which merits the use of the word? The frank answer must be that they have yet to be created.

This is the justification for speech where speech is difficult and, but for this reason, intrusive. It is futile to assert that the Church has moral guidance to offer to an age of industrial and international unrest, unless the Church can attest her claim to guide by the high moral character of her sons and daughters. It is equally futile to suppose that the living units of the Church, the men and women who accept the Christian name, can attain and sustain a high ethical standard of life unless the springs of character are constantly refreshed.

Take, for instance, Wesley's rendering of the Golden Rule : ' In all cases relating to your neighbour make his case your own,'[1] which elsewhere he explains to mean the use of ' unwearied

[1] Tenth Discourse *Upon our Lord's Sermon on the Mount.*

care to screen him from whatever might grieve or hurt his soul or body.'[1] That principle applied to industry and politics would revolutionize society. It is Christian, a just interpretation of the words of Christ : but that does not mean that the Christian's duty is discharged with the claim that the Golden Rule shall be applied to society ; he is to apply it to himself. Let him apply it intelligently to his own affairs for a single week ; in every transaction with another, in every relation to another, let him honestly try to screen his neighbour from loss and hurt, to make the other man's case his own. Temporal interest and corrupt inclination will soon be at war with the new way. Unless he is becoming a better Christian, more aware of Christ's will and the Christian resources, he will be worsted. Plainly, slackness in prayer and the study of Scripture is a costly error. Disorder in devotion means defeat in action. To be slack

[1] Sermon on *The Way to the Kingdom.*

in private is to be fickle and feeble in public.

The readiest objection is that of the busy person : ' I have no time.' This may not be thrust aside as groundless. In an age of unholy contrasts, life to one man is a holiday with occasional breaks of work ; another spends strength without ceasing in order to win the bare means to live ; a third carries burdens of responsibility from which he scarcely escapes day or night. Between the far-off days when it was written, ' It is good that a man should hope and quietly wait for the salvation of the Lord,' and the rush and pressure of life to-day, there is a great gulf fixed. That is one indictment of the modern social order ; it crowds out thinking.

Still, when the last word of objection has been urged, it remains true that compromise at this point is fatal. Prayer is vital ; knowledge of the will of God is vital. Uncompromising Christianity depends for its freshness and force on both. If the full Christian Rule of Life is to be accepted, time must be found to pray and to study the Bible. He who would be entirely Christian has no moral right to plan revolutionary designs on an unchristian world if he will not lead a revolution against his unchristian self.

Revolution is the right word. Order is to oust disorder. The occupations of the twenty-four hours are to be revised at the bidding of Christ. It is safe to begin with the conviction that the time-table of the average day ought to be recast so as to find time for devotion, and to find it early in the day. The whole armour of God is best assumed before the day's warfare begins. That may require a rescinding of certain standing-orders—or sleeping orders! Time for prayer may be won at the expense of time in bed. Certainly, to tighten up spiritual discipline will make inroads on ease, since love of ease is incompatible with earnestness.

Given a thoughtful revision of time, so that space is secured for devotion, how is it to be fruitfully occupied? The lines of reply are not to be too closely drawn. There must be room for the play of temperament ; education and occupation will go to shape the plan. Yet, under the general answer of the *Rules*, ' Family and Private Prayer ; Searching the Scriptures ; Fasting or Abstinence,' a few suggestions gleaned from experience may be gathered.

(*a*) Thoughtful Christian prayer will traverse the two spheres of rightful human aspiration, love of God and love of neighbour.

One man will find it easier to turn into speech his homage to God, Creator and Redeemer, and his own confession of unworth as a sinner. Another will more readily intercede for men, on behalf of their social needs and his own plans of service. Why should the prayer of either be left incomplete?

Unless the mind is constantly

refreshed with new thoughts and new hopes, prayer soon becomes a repetition of familiar ideas and phrases. Yet this need not be so. When Jesus taught His first disciples to pray He said, ' After this manner therefore pray ye,' and gave a form of adoration and petition. Through the nineteen centuries of Christian experience many a devout soul has cast into the mould of litany or hymn the outcry of his heart for God. This long line of religious reflection awaits our discovery, or rediscovery. It is hidden wealth which any man may make his own. Each hymnbook of the Church is really a collection of the prayers of the saints of all ages, prayer in song. It is safe to forecast that, with a return to habits of private devotion, the value of forms of prayer to assist freshness and fullness of spiritual thinking will be seen.

Let any whose range of thought of God is very limited read the timeless praises of the *Te Deum*, or such a hymn

as Newman's ' Praise to the Holiest
in the height,' or the searching words of
the Methodist Covenant Service, and a
new speech of God will dwell upon the
tongue. Let any whose knowledge of
spiritual and social necessities at
home and abroad, or whose power
to express the human needs they
know, is small, use at times a form
of intercession for all sorts and conditions of men.[1]

These are suggestions only. It is
possible to build up gradually a little
library of devotion with whose aid the
disciple at prayer can thrust thought
deeper into the hidden things of God,
and spur thought further to share the
sorrowful plight of men.

(*b*) It is good strategy to secure for
private devotion time early in the day,
it may be half an hour before break-
fast. To start the day with God is to

[1] E.g. a manual issued yearly by the Wesleyan
Methodist Missionary Society, entitled *What to Pray
for* ; and a Litany entitled *A Service of Prayer for
Social Need* (Rivington).

claim the day for God. And here is another proposal, tested and found of worth. In whatever manner prayer for one's neighbour is offered, let it include a definite naming of the people who will probably be met during the day. The Christian's neighbour is every man. The Christian's influence on human affairs to transform this evil world into a realm of God is most direct and constant on persons. Actually he is all the time redeeming or repelling men by speech and deed. Let the morning prayer include a thoughtful review of what the day is likely to hold. Duty by duty, person by person, set out the expected programme of work and leisure. It is hard to quarrel with a man for whom one has prayed ; difficult to consent to dishonour when the hour of peril has been foreseen, and the cry raised, ' Lord, save me.'

(*c*) An intimate knowledge of the Bible is priceless. The daily reading of the Scriptures is not a fetish. The

Old and New Testaments are records
of the unveiling of the will of God in
human history. Criticism of the text
of Scripture does not affect this fact ;
reverent criticism has added to our
knowledge of the way in which the
holy will was declared. Never did the
Bible so repay study as now. Scholar-
ship has illumined its meaning ; though
a man need not be a scholar to share
in the spoils which scholars have won,
since modern helps to Biblical research
abound.

Study of the Scriptures has again
and again thrust up into the light of
day convictions which have fired the
world afresh with faith and hope and
love. The first generation of Christians who spread the Faith along the
Mediterranean shores cherished the
Hebrew Scriptures, oral and written
stories of Jesus and His teaching, and
letters from the apostles. Luther's
reassertions of justification by faith
and of the priesthood of all believers,
grew out of a diligent examination of

the Psalms and the Pauline Epistles. The preaching of the Wesleys was preceded by years of close Biblical study at Oxford and in Georgia ; it was as ' one was reading Luther's preface to the Epistle to the Romans ' that John Wesley, on that notable birthnight in Aldersgate Street, felt his heart ' strangely warmed.'

We can inherit the record of our fathers' quests, but we cannot inherit the spiritual treasure they discovered and made their own. Each generation must search the field afresh, and find, and pay the price that beggars and makes rich. For this reason the Bible remains and must remain the Christian's chart and compass.

(*d*) The creation of habits of private devotion will lead to the creation or renewal of the habit of family worship where that is practicable. The family is the unit group of society. It is significant that family questions are dominating public affairs. Slumdom is attacked because it renders a whole-

some family life wellnigh impossible ;
casual employment because it makes
the provision of food and clothing
casual ; intemperance because it ruins
the home.   National wellbeing is
linked at every point with the quality
of the nation's home-life.

The Christian family should be the
normal and the closest bond between
personal religion and public righteousness. The natural expansion of the
Christian Faith is through parent to
child. Of all influences, those which
surround child-life are the most enduring. Wherever we go we carry with
us the marks of early training or
neglect ; in some things to the end of
our days we care or are careless, scruple
or are free from scruple, much as our
parents. Youth and adult years add
lessons, but life's first teachings cut
deep grooves of habit.

It is true that a child does not inherit personal religion ; that is to be
sought personally of God ; but it is
of equal truth that a child does inherit

an attitude to religion and an estimate
of religion. One gain from family
worship is that family life is hallowed
by it ; another, that where common
prayer and reading of the Scripture
is the habit of the home the Christian
Faith stakes out a claim in the coming
generation. The worshipping family
is of vital worth to the nation and the
Faith. It is a type and promise of the
race to be.

(*e*) Wesley's view of fasting is most
fully stated in the Seventh Discourse
Upon our Lord's Sermon on the Mount.
This should be read side by side with
his sermon on *Self-Denial.* For fasting,
or abstinence—that is, recourse to a
plain spare diet—was to him an outward expression of inward principle, a
principle of self-renouncing love which
ought to direct life. ' If any man will
come after Me, let him deny himself,
and take up his cross daily, and follow
Me,' is the text for the sermon on
Self-Denial. ' It is always owing to the
want either of self-denial, or taking up

his cross,' he writes, ' that any man
does not thoroughly follow Him, is not
fully a disciple of Christ.' It was as an
aid or spur to self-denial, which depends for its constancy on self-control—
or better, Christ-control—that Wesley
practised and counselled periodical
fasting.

Therefore it is with fasting as related
to character that the disciple of Jesus
has concern : an occasional abstinence
from food, private, disciplinary, prayer-
ful. Fasting ' without relation to
spiritual ends is a duty nowhere enjoined or counselled. But Christianity
hath to do with it as it may be made an
instrument of the Spirit, by subduing
the lusts of the flesh, or removing
any hindrances of religion.'[1] That is
the tenor of Jesus' teaching.[2] These
are the two legitimate aims : a man
may fast to cleanse himself from
all defilement of flesh and spirit ;
and he may fast to prepare himself

[1] Jeremy Taylor, *Holy Living*, chap. iv. section v.
[2] Note especially Matt. vi. 16-18.

for a choice or duty of especial gravity.

The first purpose includes the banishment of ' that gay inattention to things of the deepest concern ' to which some natures are prone, and particularly the conquest of unchaste thought, desire, and act. ' All my senses have been windows to let sin in,' cried Jeremy Taylor ; a like confession will be made by most honest hearts. In such hours, to bring the body into subjection is to restore the primacy of the soul. ' Here,' says Wesley, ' is another perpetual reason for fasting ; to remove the food of lust and sensuality, to withdraw the incentives of foolish and hurtful desires, of vile and vain affections.'

Of the second purpose, the momentous call of Barnabas and Saul for the foreign field is an early Christian example. As the prophets and teachers of the little Church at Antioch ' ministered to the Lord and fasted,' the great call came. With fast and prayer the Church sent the missionaries on their

adventurous way. It may be that
thus the vision splendid will come to
companies of disciples who to-day keep
vigil with Jesus.

CHAPTER VI

' THIS STRANGE SIGHT, A CHRISTIAN WORLD '

L

According to His promise, we look for new heavens and a new earth, wherein dwelleth righteousness.

Wherefore, beloved, seeing that ye look for these things, give diligence that ye may be found in peace, without spot and blameless in His sight.

The Second Epistle General of Peter.

CHAPTER VI

'THIS STRANGE SIGHT, A CHRISTIAN WORLD'

I

THERE is a curious tract by Wesley in which he discusses a 'short and sure method' for the conversion of Ireland to Protestant Christianity.[1] Since Roman Catholics venerate the holy lives of the apostles, 'let all the clergy of the Church of Ireland,' he says, 'only live like the apostles and preach like the apostles, and the thing is done.'

Give the saying a wider range. Let it apply to the new paganism which in this wealthy age enthrones the body

[1] *A Short Method of Converting all the Roman Catholics in the Kingdom of Ireland.*

but enslaves the soul. How is the
Church to restore the primacy of the
soul, to dethrone Mammon, to proclaim
Christ Sovereign by right and by consent ? How is the kingdom of the world
to become the kingdom of our Lord ?
There is a sure method. Let the sons
and daughters of the Church live like
the apostles ; find and follow, as they
did, a ' Way ' of simple Christian goodness. ' Open your hearts to us ; we
wronged no man, we corrupted no
man, we took advantage of no man,'
wrote Paul.[1] That was apostolic doctrine and practice. That is what it
means to live like apostles. Sermons
and speeches and statements of creed
must bear the signature of an honest
life, or this age scorns them, and it is all
to the good that it should do so.

Hence the radical importance of the
inquiry with which our quest began,
What is the true Rule of Life for the
modern disciple of Jesus ? The answer
has been sought in a study of the Rule

[1] 2 Cor. vii. 2.

of Life framed by the early Methodists
in the eighteenth century, in a social
situation in certain respects strangely
like our own. Over against the evil
most generally practised in their day,
profanity and drunkenness, violence
and smuggling, love of money and love
of show, they set the Christian Negative,
' doing no harm.' Over against a self-
centred, self-indulging manner of life
that forgot the bodily needs of the poor
and ignored the spiritual rights of all,
they placed the Christian Positive,
' doing good.' In face of the supposed
impossibility of obeying a Rule of Life
so constant and so comprehending, they
searched out the source of an unearthly
energy and found it in the Christian
Dynamic, an enriching contact with
Christ through ' the ordinances of
God.'

Thus they triumphed, and thus may
we. There is no principle asserted in
the ' Rules of the Society of the People
called Methodists ' to which the Christian confessors of the twentieth century

do not owe obedience. Specific modes of obedience vary from generation to generation, but the principles which shape the obediences of the Christian do not vary, because they are Christian principles. To cite one case : the law of social honesty was broken in the eighteenth century by smuggling, the deliberate evasion of taxes ; the law of social honesty is broken in the twentieth century by sweating, the deliberate underpayment of the wage-earner. The writ of Christ as King runs through all centuries, in all countries, and governs all circumstances. Loyal and loving obedience to Christ in all things is the summit of character ; it is that Christian Perfection which the primitive Methodists joyously proclaimed, and the manner of which—in outward deed and inward devotion—the *Rules* define.

William Law, whose treatise *On Christian Perfection* strongly influenced Wesley, defined Christian Perfection as ' the right performance of our necessary duties,' consisting not ' in any singular state or condition of life, or in any particular set of duties, but in the holy and religious conduct of ourselves in every state of life.' Elsewhere he put it, ' They only renounce the world as they ought who live in the midst of it without worldly tempers, who comply with their share in the offices of the world, without complying with the spirit that reigneth in the world.' Wesley anchored his repeated expositions of Christian Perfection to the great sayings of Scripture. His final, considered statement of the type of character for which the *Rules* stand is this[1]: ' A Methodist is one who loves the Lord his God with all his heart, with all his soul, with all his mind, and with all his strength. . . . And loving God, he loves his neighbour as himself ; he loves every man as his own soul.' That language is faithful to the unvarying teaching of the New Testament. ' It is the doctrine of St.

[1] *A Plain Account of Christian Perfection*, 1777.

Paul, the doctrine of St. James, of St.
Peter, and St. John, and no otherwise
Mr. Wesley's than as it is the doctrine
of every one who preaches the pure
and the whole gospel ! ' It describes
essential thorough-going Christianity
in every age, the Christianity that
conquers.

II

But what is to be the area of its
conquest ? If Christian men live by
this Rule, is it for their own sakes or has
their way of living a social value ? Is
there a perfection of society as well as a
perfection of the individual ? In a
word, what is the good life to effect ?
In 1744 John Wesley preached a
notable sermon on ' Scriptural Christianity,' in St. Mary's, Oxford, before
the University in which he was himself
a Fellow. After treating first, of
Christianity ' As beginning to exist in
individuals,' next ' As spreading from
one to another,' in the third place he

considers it ' As covering the earth.'
' Let us stand a little,' he says, ' and
survey this strange sight, *a Christian
world* ! ' He recalls Isaiah's glowing
words concerning latter days when
' the earth shall be full of the knowledge
of God, as the waters cover the sea ' ;
and Paul's supreme assurance that
human blindness and hardening would
some day be overpast, ' the fullness of
the Gentiles ' would come in, and ' all
Israel ' be saved.[1] Then, true to his
practical bent, he adds scripture to
scripture to show that a Christian
world must mean a world from which
inequity and hate and lust are banished,
and where righteousness is no longer
singular but social, governing all. The
conflicts of the peoples would die away :
' nation shall not lift up sword against
nation, neither shall they learn war any
more.' Civil discord would be at an
end ; for no extortion would ' grind
the face of the poor.' Destitution

[1] The passages cited are Isa. ii. 2, 4 ; xi. 6–9, 10–12 ;
lx. 1, 16–19, 21 ; and Rom. xi. 1, 11, 12, 25, 26.

would disappear ; none would lack,
for every one would love his neighbour
as himself, and all walk by the one
rule, ' Whatsoever ye would that men
should do unto you, even so do unto
them.' England might be far from
a Christian country, Oxford remote
from the character of a Christian city,
yet this man saved by the grace of
Jesus knew that the race would be
saved by that grace.

Nothing could shatter such confi-
dence. In 1758, when the Seven
Years' War was at its height, with
France and Austria leagued against
England and Prussia, and central
Europe and Canada and India one vast
field of battle, Charles Wesley wrote
*Hymns of Intercession for all Man-
kind.* He sang :

> Our earth we now lament to see
>   With floods of wickedness o'erflowed,
> With violence, wrong, and cruelty,
>   One wide extended field of blood,
> Where men like fiends each other tear
> In all the hellish rage of war.

From man's hellish rage his appeal rose
to God :

> Oh, might the Universal Friend
>   This havoc of His creatures see !
> Bid our unnatural discord end ;
>   Declare us reconciled to Thee ;
> Write kindness on our inward parts,
> And chase the murderer from our hearts !

Faith overleapt the bitter years of
strife. The day must come when
violence should no more be heard in the
land, neither wasting nor destruction.
So in that black hour the song of the
dauntless singer mounted again to
God, the Universal Friend :

> Father of everlasting love,
>   To every soul Thy Son reveal,
> Our guilt and sufferings to remove,
>   Our deep, original wound to heal ;
> And bid the fallen race arise,
> And turn our earth to paradise.

That is the vision eternal, the glory
that excelleth. ' There shall be no
more curse.' All earth's unnatural

discords shall have ending. A fallen race shall rise, a blighted world return to beauty.

The things that John the Apostle saw in the isle that is called Patmos are the ultimately true. All the iniquities of all the ages were gathered into one city, the Babylon of his dream, a strong city and great. Yet the doom even of Babylon was spoken, and the smoke of her burning went up ; for Babylon the Mighty had fallen, and her traffic in the souls of men ceased. Then John beheld Jerusalem, the new and holy, coming down out of heaven from God, the city which hath foundations and shall endure. Sin, and the sorrows born of sin, were thrust without its walls. God shall tabernacle with men, a great voice out of the throne declared, and they shall be His peoples and He their God ; He shall wipe away every tear from their eyes, neither shall there be mourning nor crying nor pain any more. As in heaven, so on earth, shall the Holy Will be done.

III

The characteristic of Wesley's teaching is that it links the present age, scarred and stained and sorrowful, with the tearless age that is to be.

In the University Sermon he turns from the picture of Christianity ' covering the earth,' and arraigns the living men before him. ' Where does this Christianity now exist? Where, I pray, do the Christians live? . . . It is utterly needful that some one should use great plainness of speech toward you. . . . Let us confess we have never yet seen a Christian country upon earth.' What, for example, of Oxford where he preached? ' Is this city a Christian city? Are all the Magistrates, all Heads and Governors of Colleges and Halls, and their respective Societies —not to speak of the inhabitants of the town—of one heart and soul? Is the love of God shed abroad in our hearts? And are our lives agreeable thereto? ' So in turn he questions Fellows,

Students, and Scholars, fearlessly unmasking the gay, idle sensual life of his day, and calling them boldly to repentance. If the city were to be of noble character there must be noble citizens.

The one sure hope of the better age is the better man, made better by the renewing grace of Jesus. Let the better man become the well-instructed man, knowing the full Christian Rule and keeping it, and with him the better age begins ; for Christ's new man is to be a herald of Christ's new world, making ready the way of the Lord, making His paths straight.

That, in briefest terms, is the message of Wesley, as valid to-day as when first spoken. A scheme to reconstruct society which ignored the redemption of the individual was unthinkable to him ; a doctrine to save sinning men, with no aim to transform them into crusaders against social sin was equally unthinkable. The disciple-company of Jesus must make war on the paganism of the age and all its works. For that cause the Christian is to live, in that campaign to die ; there is no quittance from this warfare.

However grave the challenge of the passing hour, however fierce the strife, the issue of the age-long conflict is not in question. The triumph of Christ is assured. The coming age is the age of Jesus. What eye hath not seen shall yet stand in splendour upon earth, the living City of God ; and the toils and the strifes and the prayers of the servants of God go to its building. In Peter's glowing phrase, Christ is the Corner-stone of the Zion that is to be, and they that love Him are built as living stones into that spiritual house, the temple of humanity redeemed.

APPENDIX

THE FULL TEXT OF THE RULES OF THE SOCIETY OF THE PEOPLE CALLED METHODISTS

1. In the latter end of the year 1739, eight or ten persons came to me in London, who appeared to be deeply convinced of sin, and earnestly groaning for redemption. They desired (as did two or three more the next day) that I would spend some time with them in prayer, and advise them how to flee from the wrath to come, which they saw continually hanging over their heads. That we might have more time for this great work, I appointed a day when they might all come together; which, from thenceforward, they did every week; viz. on Thursday, in the evening. To these, and as many more as desired to join with them (for their number increased daily), I gave those advices from time to time which I judged most needful for them; and we always concluded our meeting with prayer suited to their several necessities.

2. This was the rise of the UNITED SOCIETY, first in London, and then in other places. Such a Society is no other than ' *a company of men* having the form, and seeking the power, *of godliness ; united, in order to pray together, to receive the word of exhortation, and to watch over one another in love, that they may help each other to work out their salvation.*'

3. That it may the more easily be discerned whether they are indeed working out their own salvation, each Society is divided into smaller companies, called Classes, according to their respective places of abode. There are about twelve persons in every Class ; one of whom is styled the *Leader.* It is his business,—

(1) To see each person in his Class once a week at least, in order

To inquire how their souls prosper ;

To advise, reprove, comfort, or exhort as occasion may require ;

To receive what they are willing to give towards the support of the gospel :

(2) To meet the Ministers and the Stewards of the Society once a week in order

To inform the Minister of any that are sick, or of any that walk disorderly, and will not be reproved ;

To pay to the Stewards what they have

M

received of their several Classes in the
week preceding; and

To show their account of what each
person has contributed.

4. There is only one condition pre-
viously required in those who desire admission into these Societies; viz. '*a
desire to flee from the wrath to come, to be
saved from their sins.*' But wherever this is
really fixed in the soul it will be shown
by its fruits. It is therefore expected of
all who continue therein, that they should
continue to evidence their desire of
salvation,

FIRST, By doing no harm, by avoiding
evil in every kind; especially that which
is most generally practised. Such is

The taking the name of God in vain;

The profaning the day of the Lord,
either by doing ordinary work thereon, or by buying or selling;

Drunkenness; *buying* or *selling spirituous liquors*, or *drinking them*, unless
in cases of extreme necessity;

Fighting, quarrelling, brawling; brother
going to law with brother; returning
evil for evil, or *railing for railing;* the
using many words in buying or selling;

The *buying* or *selling uncustomed goods;*

The *giving or taking things on usury;*
i.e. unlawful interest;

Uncharitable or *unprofitable* conversation ; particularly speaking evil of magistrates or of ministers ;

Doing to others as we would not they should do unto us ;

Doing what we know is not for the glory of God ; as—

The *putting on of gold or costly apparel ;*

The *taking such diversions* as cannot be used in the name of the LORD JESUS ;

The *singing* those *songs,* or *reading* those *books* which do not tend to the knowledge or love of GOD ;

Softness, and needless self-indulgence :

Laying up treasures upon earth ;

Borrowing without a probability of paying ; or taking up goods without a probability of paying for them.

5. It is expected of all who continue in these Societies, that they should continue to evidence their desire of salvation,

SECONDLY, By doing good, by being in every kind merciful after their power ; as they have opportunity, doing good of every possible sort, and as far as is possible, to all men ;

To their bodies, of the ability that God giveth, by giving food to the hungry, by clothing the naked, by visiting or helping them that are sick or in prison ;

To their souls, by instructing, *reproving*,
or exhorting all they have any intercourse with ; trampling under foot
that enthusiastic doctrine of devils,
that ' we are not to do good, unless
our heart be free to it.'

By doing good especially to them that
are of the household of faith, or groaning so to be ; employing them preferably to others, buying one of another,
helping each other in business ; and
so much the more, because the world
will love its own, and them *only.*

By all possible *diligence* and *frugality*,
that the gospel be not blamed.

By running with patience the race that
is set before them, *denying themselves,
and taking up their cross daily ;* submitting to bear the reproach of Christ ;
to be as the filth and offscouring
of the world ; and looking that men
should *say all manner of evil of them
falsely, for the Lord's sake.*

6. It is expected of all who desire to
continue in these Societies, that they should
continue to evidence their desire of salvation,

THIRDLY, By attending upon all the
ordinances of GOD ; such are,

The public worship of God ;

The ministry of the word, either read or
expounded ;

The Supper of the Lord ;
Family and private prayer ;
Searching the Scriptures ; and
Fasting or abstinence.

7. These are the General Rules of our Societies : all which we are taught of God to observe, even in His written word, the only rule, and the sufficient rule, both of our faith and practice. And all these we know His Spirit writes on every truly awakened heart. If there be any among us who observe them not, who habitually break any of them, let it be made known unto them who watch over that soul, as they that must give an account. We will admonish him of the error of his ways : we will bear with him for a season. But then if he repent not, he hath no more place among us. We have delivered our own souls.

JOHN WESLEY.

May 1, 1743.   CHARLES WESLEY.

Southampton Times Co., Ltd
Printers and Bookbinders,
70 Above Bar, Southampton.